Companion to the Lec

## 1. Prefaces to the Lessons

David Calvert and John Stacey

# Companion to the Lectionary

## 1. Prefaces to the Lessons

EPWORTH PRESS

*7162 0363 4*

*Photoset by Input Typesetting Ltd*
*and printed in Great Britain by*
*The Camelot Press Ltd*
*London and Southampton*

# Contents

# Contents

# Foreword

In the writing of these prefaces, designed to be read before the lessons in churches where the lectionary of either *The Methodist Service Book* or *The Alternative Service Book 1980* is in use, the text to which reference has been made is that of the Revised Standard Version.

We are grateful for liturgical advice from the Rev. Neil Dixon and for a large typing operation by Mrs Diane Walker and Mrs Gladys Handley of the Methodist Local Preachers' Office.

*December 1981*                                        David Calvert
                                                       John Stacey

# Abbreviations

MSB     *The Methodist Service Book*
ASB     *The Alternative Service Book 1980*

# The Christian Year

The Christian Year is divided into two parts. The first is dominated by the great festivals of Christmas and Easter. Each of these festivals is preceded by a number of weeks set aside for preparation and is followed by a number of weeks during which its message is further explored.

The Christmas cycle begins on the Ninth Sunday before Christmas, reaches its climax on Christmas Day, and continues throughout the season of Epiphany.

The Easter cycle begins on the Ninth Sunday before Easter, reaches its climax on Easter Day, and continues throughout the six Sundays after Easter.

During this first part of the Christian Year, attention is focused on Jesus Christ: the preparation for him in the Old Testament, his birth and public ministry, his passion and death, his resurrection and ascension.

The second part of the Christian Year begins at Pentecost and continues until the Christmas cycle restarts. During this period, themes relating to the life of the individual Christian and of the Christian church are explored.

**The Sundays before Christmas**
Christianity developed out of the religion of the Jewish people, and the Christian tradition has always recognized in the Old Testament the background to the work of Jesus Christ as well as an important collection of books in its own right. During this first period of the Christian Year, therefore, attention is focused on some major themes of the Old Testament which explore the relationship between God, Creator and Redeemer, and his people. In the two weeks immediately preceding Christmas, John the Baptist (depicted in the Gospels as the forerunner of Jesus) and Mary the mother of Jesus claim attention.

**Christmas Day and the Sundays after Christmas**
After nine Sundays of preparation, the Christmas cycle reaches its climax on Christmas Day, when the birth of Christ is celebrated.

The lessons of the next two Sundays include stories concerned with Jesus as an infant and a child.

## Epiphany and the Sundays after Epiphany
Epiphany means 'manifestation', and the traditional themes for this season (beginning with the Wise Men on the feast day itself, though this theme is now, in the Methodist Church, more often associated with the Sunday after Christmas) seek to show forth Jesus' nature as Son of God and Revealer of God.

## The Sundays before Easter and Holy Week
The first three weeks link the Christmas cycle, which is ending, with the Easter cycle, which is beginning. They concentrate upon Christ as healer and worker of miracles, roles in which his divine ministry was fulfilled. Yet because these aspects of Jesus' ministry earned him the hatred of the Jewish leaders, these themes also point towards the Cross, as do the themes of the other Sundays before Easter. These weeks are a preparation for Good Friday and Easter Day through meditation upon the work of Christ in terms of temptation, conflict, suffering, transfiguration, the victory of the Cross and the way of the Cross. On Maundy Thursday and Good Friday respectively, the themes are the Upper Room and the Death of Christ.

## Easter Day to the Sixth Sunday after Easter
The great theme of the resurrection of Jesus is celebrated on Easter Day and continues to dominate the Easter cycle, which concludes with the Ascension. The first four Sundays after Easter are associated in the first year with the resurrection appearances of Jesus and in the second year with some of his 'I am' sayings, recorded in the Fourth Gospel.

## Pentecost to the Twenty-third Sunday after Pentecost
The Christmas and Easter cycles have recorded God's mighty acts in creation and in the life, death, resurrection and ascension of Jesus Christ. Pentecost, the third major Christian festival, adds the story of the gift of the Holy Spirit. The themes of the first part of the Christian Year are gathered together on the Sunday after Pentecost (Trinity Sunday) when the doctrine of the Holy Trinity is proclaimed. The Sundays after Pentecost constitute the second part of the Christian Year; their themes are concerned with aspects of the life of the Christian community and of the individual Christian, led by the Holy Spirit.

# Notes on the Use of the Prefaces

1. For every Sunday, and some weekdays, Prefaces are provided for the lessons in *The Methodist Service Book*, followed by Prefaces for the lessons in *The Alternative Service Book 1980*. All references under ASB are to Prefaces provided for the lessons in *The Methodist Service Book*, unless otherwise stated. In cases where an ASB lesson is a few verses longer or shorter than the corresponding MSB lesson, the MSB Preface is used only if appropriate. Otherwise a separate ASB Preface is given.

2. Sometimes the lectionaries supply the option of a longer or shorter lesson from a particular book. In such cases, the Preface always applies to the shorter version.

3. Prefaces are intended to help congregations better to understand the lessons. It is recommended that the preacher or reader prepares for the reading of the Prefaces as carefully as he prepares for the reading of the lessons themselves. The Prefaces can be used flexibly, according to need and situation.

4. When, in the Lord's Supper or Holy Communion, an ascription is said by the congregation after the announcement of the Gospel, it is suggested either that the Preface be omitted, or that it be read before the Gospel is announced.

# Ninth Sunday before Christmas
(Fifth before Advent)

*The Creation*

### First year, morning

*Genesis 1.1–3,24–31a*
This passage is taken from the first of the two creation stories found in the book of Genesis. (The second is in Chapter 2.) In this account, creation proceeds in stages: beginning from the void and culminating in the creation of man; in the other account, man is created first, out of dust. Here, all creation is seen to be good, and man is given special responsibility as guardian of creation.

*Colossians 1.15–20*
In this hymn in praise of Christ, Paul speaks chiefly of Christ's relationship to the created order, describing him as both the beginning and the climax of all creation. In making these claims about Christ, Paul is echoing Jewish thought about the creative activity, or wisdom, of God. He is led to make such large claims for Christ because he sees in him the fullness of God himself.

*John 1.1–14*
In this prologue to the Gospel, the writer refers to creation in order to relate the historical life of Jesus to the whole purpose of God. Because Jesus expresses God's nature he is called the Word of God. This term was associated in Judaism with the creative activity of God and with wisdom, and in the Greek world with meaning and purpose. These understandings are focused in Christ.

### First year, evening

*Proverbs 8.1,22–31*
In this passage the voice of wisdom herself speaks. The image of wisdom was frequently used in later Jewish thought to express the relationship of God to his creation. Although its use owes much to the contact Israel had with other cultures and religions, it developed a distinctive meaning: God's wisdom became associated with the

*1*

Jewish law, with God's word, with the spirit of God, and eventually, in Christian thought, with Christ.

*Revelation 21.15–27*
The prophet describes his vision of the new Jerusalem, giving in detail its size and the materials used in its construction. The special feature of this symbolic city is that there is no temple there; its place has been taken by the presence of Christ himself. The city is to be a dwelling place for the righteous people of all the nations.

## Second year, morning

*Genesis 2.4b–9, 15–25*
This passage is taken from the second of the two creation stories found in the book of Genesis. The first story speaks of creation in stages, culminating in the creation of man. Here, God creates man first, by shaping him out of dust and breathing into him the breath of life. Everything else in creation is made for man, and finally, woman is created out of his body. The reference to man being forbidden to eat from the tree of the knowledge of good and evil implies that man must not attempt to usurp the position of God.

*Revelation 4.1–11*
The author of the book of Revelation, a Christian prophet, describes in this chapter his vision of the worship of God in heaven. The passage belongs to a type of literature which uses traditional, vivid images to express symbolically a message that could not be written openly, for fear of persecution.

*John 3.1–8*
Nicodemus, a leading Jew, comes to Jesus seeking the kingdom of God. In this story, Nicodemus is treated as a representative of the Jews, and so the conversation is presented as part of the debate between the church and Judaism. When Jesus says he must be born anew, Nicodemus fails to understand that he means a renewal of human life by God's Spirit, as later expressed by the church in baptism.

**Second year, evening**

*Job 38.1–18*
Job, afflicted in many ways, has not been convinced by the arguments of his friends that he must acknowledge his sin and repent, but has insisted on his right to meet God. Here God speaks to Job about the wonder of creation, and Job is confronted with his own ignorance. The passage refers to the mysterious nature of the sea, which in Hebrew thought often represented hostility to God: God's control of the waters of the world is therefore the clearest indication of his sovereignty.

*Acts 14.8–17*
This story records how Paul and Barnabas heal a crippled man. The crowd's reaction is to hail them as Zeus, king of the gods, and Hermes, messenger of the gods. There follows a speech typical of Jewish preaching to Gentiles, for there is no specific mention of Christ. It condemns idolatry and declares that God the creator has made himself known through the blessings of nature.

ASB
Prefaces as above.

# Eighth Sunday before Christmas
(Fourth before Advent)

*The Fall*

**First year, morning**

*Genesis 3.1–15*
This is the story of man's temptation to seek equality with God. The sin of mankind is portrayed through the story of the serpent who deceives the woman and, through her, the man. As a result, the garden of Eden is lost. Through this act of disobedience the relationship between man and God is broken, and the breach affects the whole created order.

*Romans 7.7–12*
Paul is writing about the close relationship beween sin and the Jewish law. In an illustration reminiscent of Adam eating the forbidden fruit, Paul comments on his own life as a Jew, recalling how the command not to covet caused him to covet, and he argues that, in this sense, the law encourages sin. Yet Paul still claims that the law is good, for its function is to reveal sin for what it is.

*John 3.13–21*
The conversation between Jesus and Nicodemus has led into a statement by the writer of this Gospel about the purpose of the coming of Christ: as the Son of God, he has come from God to bring salvation to all who believe in him. The writer returns to the image of light and darkness, used in the first chapter, to illustrate how the coming of Christ brings both salvation and judgment.

**First year, evening**

*Isaiah 44.6–17*
This passage is one of the clearest expressions of the prophet's belief that there is only one God. It echoes the insistence of the book of Deuteronomy that Israel should abandon all other cults and worship God alone. This prophetic word is emphasized by a vivid image illustrating the folly of worshipping idols, mere human creations, instead of God, the divine creator.

*I Corinthians 10.1–13*
In a passage which draws on the experience of the Israelites in the wilderness, Paul warns the Corinthian Christians that even the sacraments will not guarantee salvation. Baptism and the Lord's Supper are likened to the Israelites' experience of receiving food and drink in the desert. Paul interprets Jewish scripture in the light of Christ's coming and uses it to warn Christians against idolatry and immorality, the temptations which are now facing the Corinthians.

## Second year, morning

*Genesis 4.1–10*
This passage comes immediately after the account of the expulsion of Adam and Eve from the garden of Eden because they have disobeyed God's will. The breach in the relationship between man and God results in a breakdown in human relationships, illustrated by the murder of Abel. This story signifies the beginning of humanity's open rebellion against the rule of God.

*I John 3.9–18*
The writer is seeking to distinguish between those who belong to the true Christian community and those who do not and the test is that of brotherly love. Unlike Cain, Christians as children of God do not commit sin: genuine fellowship with Jesus Christ prevents this. What may appear to be an exaggeration in the first verse must be seen as a protest against opponents who argued that sin was permissible because it gave scope for God's grace.

*Mark 7.14–23*
Jesus has been defending his disciples against the charge of ritual uncleanness brought against them by the Pharisees. Here he makes it clear that outward things cannot cause inward uncleanness. To Mark, the clear implication of this principle is that there can be no distinction between clean and unclean food, an important issue in the life of the early church.

## Second year, evening

*Jeremiah 17.5–14*
This passage is part of the prophet Jeremiah's denunciation of Israel's sin in rejecting God. God alone is able to save. The man

who trusts in himself is doomed, but the man who trusts in God is secure. The prophet is therefore anxious that the people should return to the recognition and worship of God.

*Romans 5.12–19*
To appreciate the meaning of this passage it is necessary to understand that Paul believed Adam to be a historical person through whose sinful act sin and death became the lot of his descendants. As part of his description of what God has done for Christians, Paul contrasts Adam and Christ: one brought death, the other brings life. He then contrasts Moses and Christ: the law under Moses brought condemnation, for it was not kept, but the gift of grace experienced in Christ brings fellowship with God.

## ASB
Prefaces for first and second years are transposed.

# Seventh Sunday before Christmas
(Third before Advent)

*The Election of God's People: Abraham*

### First year, morning

*Genesis 12.1–9*
This passage tells how Abraham is called to leave his own country. It is a story both of God's promise and of Abraham's faith: God promises that Abraham will be the beginning of a great people; Abraham shows his faith by setting out in obedience to God's command.

*Romans 4.13–25*
Paul reminds his readers of the account of Abraham's faith found in the book of Genesis, and uses it to illustrate the faith that Christians should have. Abraham accepted what God had promised, and God responded by treating Abraham as a righteous man. For Paul, it is significant that this happened before the law was given: faith and response are therefore independent of the law.

*John 8.51–58*
The writer of John's Gospel relates an incident of conflict between Jesus and the Jews in which Jesus, by the use of the words 'I am', claims for himself an authority greater than that of Abraham. The story is used to support the claim that the Christian church is the true people of God; because Christians are obedient to Jesus, God gives them eternal life.

### First year, evening

*Isaiah 29.13–24*
The prophet Isaiah rebukes those whose worship of God is only a formality, and expresses the sure hope that God will act again in history, as he did with Abraham, to convince the people of his power. This passage therefore attacks those who rely on their own abilities: probably in this case, those who seek to save the nation through an alliance with Egypt. The prophet believes strongly in God's power to transform his people.

*Romans 9.1–8*
Paul seeks to justify God's treatment of the Jews. He argues that God's word has not been broken, for the promises he made to the children of Israel have been fulfilled in those who belong to Christ. Paul, who is clearly grieved at the way in which the Jews have rejected Christ, reveals here his own inner conflict: he belongs both to the Jewish people, to whom the promises were made, and to the Christian community, which has now inherited God's blessings. Later in the letter, Paul tries to resolve this tension through the hope that eventually all Israel will be saved.

## Second year, morning

*Genesis 22.1–18*
The story of the offering of Isaac, dramatically told, is used by the writer to illustrate the supreme test in Abraham's spiritual development. Abraham stands the test by his complete surrender to God's will. Some scholars believe the story to be a justification of Israel's rejection of the custom of human sacrifice.

*James 2.14–24*
James is protesting against the claim of some Christians that faith on its own can save man. That is why Martin Luther, who made much of being saved 'by faith alone', did not care for this epistle. James, however, insists that faith must show itself in action, and he uses the story of Abraham's willingness to sacrifice Isaac as an illustration for his argument.

*Luke 20.9–16*
Luke records a parable warning the Jews that, because of their unfaithfulness, they may lose the inheritance they claim as descendants of Abraham. The parable uses a common image of Israel as God's vineyard: the heir in the story is Jesus and the tenants who kill him are the Jews. The destruction of the faithless Jews seems to refer to the destruction of Jerusalem by the Romans in AD 70.

## Second year, evening

*Genesis 13.1–18*
As a result of conflict between their herdsmen, Abraham invites Lot to choose which part of the land he wants, and Lot selects the fertile

Jordan valley. It seems as if Abraham has a bad bargain, but it is to him and his descendants that God undertakes to give what is aptly called 'the promised land'.

*Galatians 3.1–14*
Paul challenges the Galatian Christians to remain true to the gospel by appealing to their own initial experience. They responded to Christ not through obedience to the Jewish law but through faith, just as Abraham, the father of the Jewish people, had responded to God. For Paul, this emphasis upon faith rather than obedience to the law opens the way for the Christian gospel to be preached to Gentiles, the issue which causes the conflict reflected in this passage.

ASB
Prefaces as above.

# Sixth Sunday before Christmas
(Second before Advent)

*The Promise of Redemption: Moses*

**First year, morning**

*Exodus 3.1–15*
The story of the burning bush describes Moses' encounter with God.
He calls Moses to secure the freedom of the people, so that his
promises can be fulfilled and the Israelites brought into the promised
land. To Moses, God declares his name – Yahweh, I AM. The exact
meaning of this term is unclear, but it indicates to Moses something
of the mysterious nature of the God whom he is called to serve.

*Hebrews 3.1–6*
The writer of the letter to the Hebrews compares Jesus with Moses.
Both were faithful; but whereas Moses was a servant in God's house,
Jesus is the son of the house and therefore has the greater honour.
This comparison is made to show that Jesus is not just a second
Moses, and that the Christian faith is superior to Judaism.

*John 6.27–35*
Following his account of the feeding of the five thousand, the writer
of John's Gospel describes Jesus as the bread of life. He claims that
Jesus is superior to Moses and that he has a special relationship with
God. The people are therefore called upon to believe in Jesus as
God's revelation of himself, a major theme in this Gospel.

**First year, evening**

*Deuteronomy 18.15–22*
The writer has been warning the people not to adopt the practices of
the Canaanites nor to listen to their false prophets. The true prophet
will proclaim the word of God faithfully, rather than speak on his
own authority. The writer, anxious to help the people to distinguish
between true and false prophets, suggests that the words of the true
prophet will be fulfilled. Study of the prophetic writings, however
shows how difficult it is to apply this standard.

*Acts 3.1–26*
Peter and John are here described as able to perform a miracle comparable to those of Jesus. Such a miracle is a sign that the power of God is at work in the followers of Jesus and indicates that the new age has come. In the sermon that follows, Peter appeals to Jewish scripture to explain the suffering and death of Jesus and identifies Jesus as the prophet foretold in Deuteronomy.

## Second year, morning

*Exodus 6.2–8*
This is one of two accounts of the call of Moses and God's revelation of his name, Yahweh. This passage speaks of the call and revelation taking place in Egypt and describes God's relationship with his people in terms of a covenant. Yahweh has made a covenant with the ancestors of Moses and he renews this same covenant with him, promising deliverance from Egypt and the gift of the promised land.

*Hebrews 11.17–29*
The writer recalls the faith of the fathers of Israel, especially, in this passage, the faith of Moses. Moses is commended because he chose to accept the insecurity of his own people rather than enjoy the pleasures of Pharaoh's house. The writer describes the various stages in the story of the deliverance of the Israelites from the Egyptians as acts of faith, and he interprets Moses's motive as suffering for Christ.

*Mark 13.5–13*
This passage is part of a collection of sayings characterized by vivid imagery and a concern for future events. Mark lists certain common expectations of what will happen at the end of the world, but states that these are only the beginning of the end. The disciples must be prepared for persecution, when they will be called to witness to the truth of the gospel. The encouragement given would have special meaning for Christians in the early church suffering persecution.

## Second year, evening

*Exodus 2.1–10*
In this story of the birth and rescue of Moses, the baby is saved by being put in the river, the very manner of death prescribed by the

Pharaoh for every male Hebrew child. The story illustrates how Moses, the future deliverer of the Israelites, fulfils two essential qualifications: first, he is completely one with his own people, being fed by his own Jewish mother; second, he is a person to whom later the Pharaoh will listen because he has been brought up as an Egyptian in the Pharaoh's house.

## Hebrews 8.1–12
The writer of the letter to the Hebrews sums up his argument for the superiority of Christianity over Judaism: Christ is a superior high priest who exercises his ministry in heaven. This truth means that the old covenant under Moses is virtually obsolete, for the new covenant, prophesied by Jeremiah, has been fulfilled in Christ.

### ASB
Prefaces as above.

# Fifth Sunday before Christmas
(The Sunday before Advent)

## *The Remnant of Israel*

### First year, morning

*1 Kings 19.9–18*
After his victory over the prophets of Baal on Mount Carmel, Elijah flees from Jezebel's threats to kill him and is found alone on Mount Horeb. The prophet is full of self-pity, thinking that he alone is faithful to God. He expects God to appear to him in some dramatic way to vindicate him, but God speaks to him only in the silence. Elijah learns that there is further work for him to do and that others besides himself have remained faithful to God.

*Romans 11.13–24*
Paul warns the Gentile Christians at Rome not to presume on God's favours, reminding them that God's plan for the salvation of the world includes the Jews too. Through the analogy of the olive tree, he reminds the Gentile Christians that they are grafted branches which can be broken off under the judgment of God. At the same time, the Jews can be grafted back into the tree. Paul stresses that it is only by the kindness of God that Gentile Christians have become the successors of Israel.

*Matthew 24.38–44*
This passage is part of a discourse on the themes of judgment and the end of all things. The story of Noah is recalled to illustrate the coming of Jesus, the Son of man, which will be both unexpected and divisive. When it happens, one person will be chosen and another not. Christians are therefore urged to watch and be ready, a characteristic message in the Gospel according to Matthew.

### First year, evening

*Genesis 6.5–22*
This is the account of Noah's building of the ark in obedience to God's command. According to the story, God has resolved to destroy what he has created on the earth because of its corruption,

but Noah and his family are to be saved. Judgment and promise are the twin themes of the story: destruction for the wicked and the making of a new covenant relationship with Noah.

*Luke 12.1–7*
Jesus warns his disciples against the hypocrisy to be seen in the Pharisees. God, who sees all, is the ultimate judge of what men do. Jesus then assures his disciples that they are not to be afraid, for God will be watching over them. Luke is here reminding Christians that they are not promised protection from persecution and death, but rather that God cares for them.

## Second year, morning

*Isaiah 10.20–23*
The prophet Isaiah is speaking after king Hezekiah has surrendered to Sennacherib of Assyria and become his vassal. Isaiah looks for the time when Israel will no longer be dependent on Assyria, but will trust in God. He fears that only a few, a remnant, will so trust, and that the rest of Israel will not survive the coming judgment.

*Romans 9.19–29*
Paul seeks to justify God's choice of the Gentiles by declaring that no one has the right to question God's absolute power. He quotes passages from Jewish scripture to support his view that God has consistently chosen whom he will and rejected whom he will. God is sovereign and he will continue to call only a righteous remnant. Paul understands this remnant to include both Jews and Gentiles, indeed, all who respond to God in faith.

*Mark 13.14–23*
This passage is part of a collection of sayings characterized by vivid imagery and a concern for future events. Mark describes the coming of a grave crisis in which the people are urged to flee. The passage opens with an intriguing reference to the desolating sacrilege, which, in the book of Daniel, refers to the altar erected in the temple by Antiochus Epiphanes, the king of Syria, in 168 BC. Here it may refer to the attempt by Caligula, the Roman Emperor, to set up his own statue in the temple in AD 40, or it may be a more general reference to the worship of evil.

## Second year, evening

*I Kings 17.1–16*
When king Ahab provokes God's anger by erecting an altar to Baal, the prophet Elijah tells him that he will be punished. Baal, the Canaanite god, was worshipped as a god of nature and fertility, yet here it is the God of Israel who is in control of the natural elements of dew and rain. This story about Elijah is told to illustrate the way in which God cares for his servants. When Elijah escapes from the king's anger he is fed by the ravens and then by a Phoenician woman.

*Matthew 6.24–33*
This extract from the sermon on the mount urges Christian disciples not to be over-anxious but to trust in God. He knows their needs and will provide for them. Their priority is to further the rule of God.

## ASB
Prefaces as above.

# Fourth Sunday before Christmas
(Advent 1)

---

## The Advent Hope

### First year, morning

*Isaiah 52.1–10*
In a message addressed to those Jews who remained in Jerusalem during the time of exile, the prophet affirms that God will redeem not only them but also those who are exiled in Egypt, Assyria and Babylon. The prophet speaks of God 'buying back' the people, a metaphor which illustrates his faithfulness to the covenant between him and Israel.

*I Thessalonians 5.1–11*
The Thessalonian Christians have been speculating about the second coming of Christ. The only answer Paul gives is that any such coming will be sudden and unexpected. But he assures them that they have nothing to fear if they keep spiritually awake and trust in Christ.

*Luke 21.25–33*
This passage is part of a discourse in which Luke gathers together teaching about the coming of the Son of man and writes of the signs that will indicate when this is near. The coming event is also described as the arrival of the kingdom of God: it is the time when God will rule and the faithful will be saved. This teaching continues the old prophetic hope in the day of the Lord, but now links it specifically with Christ.


### First year, evening

*Isaiah 62.6–12*
Speaking to the Jews in Jerusalem after the exile, the prophet reminds the people that he and his assistants, the watchmen, are praying that God will fulfil his promises to his people. God responds with the assurance that the people will be free from enemy attack and will enjoy the fruits of the harvest. The prophet is encouraging a perplexed community to believe that they are God's holy and redeemed people.

*Luke 12.35–43*
This passage suggests that the disciples of Jesus will be left to take care of his household until he returns from the heavenly banquet; their task is to be vigilant. There is a further illustration of the point in the householder being ready for the thief. The passage contains an indication of Peter's leadership within the early Christian community, for it appears that a particular charge is being given to him to be a faithful steward.

## Second year, morning

*Isaiah 51.4–11*
In an urgent message, the prophet proclaims to the people waiting in exile that God will soon act in righteous judgment. Those who know God will be delivered and they need not fear the future. The prophet then addresses God directly (in the verses beginning 'Awake, awake') and he prays for a new exodus and a return of the captive people to Jerusalem.

*Romans 13.8–14*
In an echo of the teaching of Jesus, Paul reminds his readers of the supreme importance of love: it is the complete fulfilment of the law. Because Paul believes that Christians are living at the end of time, he urges them to make sure that they live according to the new order of life. This means abandoning old practices and living a life united with Christ. The word 'flesh' does not refer exclusively to the physical, but to the whole of human nature when in opposition to God.

*Matthew 25.31–46*
Matthew here tells the parable of the sheep and the goats. Some understand the parable as part of Jesus's instructions to his disciples about how they should live while, in his absence, they await the coming of the Son of man. They must help those in need. Others interpret the meaning to be that the Gentiles are judged on how they treat Christians, for in treating them they are treating Christ. In either case, the parable reinforces a clear note in Matthew's Gospel that the final judgment will be on the basis of what men have, or have not, done.

*Fourth Sunday before Christmas*

## Second year, evening

*Jeremiah 31.7–14*
The prophet Jeremiah speaks a word of comfort and hope to those
who are in exile : God is going to lead them back to Jerusalem,
where he will abundantly bless them. Jeremiah pictures the rejoicing
of those who will enjoy God's blessings: they will turn from weeping
to singing. This message is not just for those who are in exile, for the
prophet wants the whole world to know what God is doing for his
people.

*I Thessalonians 1.1–10*
In a spirit of thanksgiving, Paul writes to the Christians at Thessalonica who, through the quality of their lives, have become an
example to their fellow Christians. Using the traditional language of
the Jewish expectation of the Messiah, Paul goes on to speak of
Christians waiting for God's Son from heaven. In the early years of
the church, Christians were very conscious of living in a new age,
and they expected Christ to return soon to judge and save the world.

## ASB
## Year 1

*Isaiah 52.7–10*
This is a message addressed to those Jews who had remained in
Jerusalem during the period of the exile. It comes from the exiled
Jews in Babylon and brings the promise of hope that God's rule over
Jerusalem will be made known to all the world.

Other Prefaces as above.

# Third Sunday before Christmas
(Advent 2)

*The Word of God in the Old Testament*

**First year, morning**

*Isaiah 55.1–11*
The prophet invites Jew and Gentile alike to enter into a new covenant with God. The promise made to David will now be fulfilled in a restored Israel, which will be a witness to the nations. The prophet believes that this promised salvation will be achieved through the word of God.

*Romans 15.4–13*
Paul reminds his readers that the scriptures are an encouragement to Christians. He quotes from the Psalms, Deuteronomy and Isaiah. For Paul, it is clearly important that the Jewish scriptures confirm his belief that life in Christ is open to Jew and Gentile alike.

*John 5.36–47*
The writer of John's Gospel has spoken of the testimony of John the Baptist to Jesus. Now he argues that the works of Jesus testify that the Father has sent him, and goes on to show that the Old Testament also witnesses to him. It is here that the unbelieving Jews are most in error: they examine their scriptures looking for eternal life, but fail to see that these scriptures point to Christ, who is the source of life.

**First year, evening**

*Jeremiah 26.1–13*
This account of Jeremiah's speech in the temple in 608 BC and his subsequent arrest and trial, illustrates the courage with which the prophet openly speaks his words of judgment against the temple, the city and its people. In a threat which arouses the anger of the priests, he likens the temple to Shiloh, the ancient sanctuary which was destroyed by the Philistines in the eleventh century. Jeremiah uses the opportunity of his trial to call the city to repentance, and

makes the important claim that he is fulfilling his prophetic role in speaking the word that the Lord has given him.

*II Timothy 2.8–15*
Timothy is urged to remember Christ. He is reminded of the unfettered word of God, which is the word of truth. He is encouraged by the quotation of what is probably part of a baptismal hymn, a trustworthy saying to be passed on to fellow Christians to encourage them to be faithful.

## Second year, morning

*Isaiah 64.1–5*
The prophet cries out to God, asking him to show his presence among the people and to save them from their sins. He wants God to be acknowledged not only by the Jewish people but by the other nations as well. The prayer seems to belong to the period after the exile when there were considerable difficulties in re-establishing the Jerusalem community.

*II Timothy 3.14–4.5*
The writer of this letter to Timothy upholds the Jewish scriptures as a source of strength and inspiration. Timothy is urged to turn to the scriptures so that he may be the better equipped for his ministry. Central to this ministry is the urgent task of preaching the word, especially as the time is expected when Timothy's sound teaching will go unheeded.

*Luke 4.14–21*
Luke tells the story of the visit of Jesus to the synagogue at Nazareth. He builds into this account an announcement of the mission of Jesus, understood as the fulfilment of a passage from the book of Isaiah. Jesus is shown to be the one anointed by the Spirit. The subsequent rejection of Jesus by his own people at Nazareth anticipates his rejection by the Jews, and the whole passage indicates the writer's understanding of the subsequent ministry of Jesus.

## Second year, evening

*I Kings 22.5–17*
There has been a period of peace between Syria and Israel, but now Ahab, king of Israel, is tempted to try to regain Ramoth-gilead from

the Syrians. He seeks the support of Jehoshaphat, king of Judah, who advises that the prophets should be asked for guidance. The professional prophets foretell success, and Micaiah at first agrees but, when pressed, speaks the true prophetic word. The incident is told to illustrate the difference between a true word from God and false prophecy which merely stated what people wanted to hear.

*Romans 10.5–17*
Using quotations from Jewish scripture, Paul argues that man cannot earn his own salvation through obeying the law, but only by confessing Jesus, whom God has raised from the dead, as Lord. Paul is concerned with the preaching of this gospel to Jew and Gentile alike, for he knows that people will not be able to respond to God in faith unless the word is spoken to them.

## ASB
Prefaces as above, but the Epistles for first and second years are transposed.

# Second Sunday before Christmas
(Advent 3)

## The Forerunner

### First year, morning

*Isaiah 40.1–11*
In a message of comfort, the prophet announces salvation for the Jews exiled in Babylon. God is sending a messenger to prepare the way before him. The prophet is therefore able to assure the people that when they return, God will be in Jerusalem as their king and shepherd.

*I Corinthians 4.1–5*
Paul resists the efforts of some of the Corinthian Christians to judge him, for he will only be judged by God. This passage illustrates the uneasy relationship between Paul and the Corinthian Christians.

*John 1.19–27*
The testimony of John the Baptist, which follows the prologue to John's Gospel, is partly about himself and partly about Christ. He, John, is not the Christ nor Elijah; he is but a voice witnessing to the coming of the Lord. His baptisms point to the one who is as yet unknown, the one whom later he is to describe as the lamb of God.

### First year, evening

*Malachi 4.1–6*
The prophet Malachi sees that many people choose to live wicked lives because they appear to receive no punishment for their wickedness. He speaks of a coming day of judgment, when the wicked will be punished and the righteous rewarded, and calls on the people to observe the law of Moses. The Jewish hope of a future messenger from God who would announce the Day of the Lord came to be associated with Elijah the prophet who, it was believed, had been taken up into heaven. Here, therefore, Elijah is seen as the forerunner of the Messiah.

*Matthew 3.1–12*
Matthew describes the ministry of John the Baptist, and summarizes his preaching in the same terms as the message later brought by Jesus: a call to repentance because of the nearness of the kingdom. This account emphasizes the need for the religious leaders to repent and warns them of the judgment that is coming upon the world.

## Second year, morning

*Malachi 3.1–5*
The prophet Malachi has rejected the people's suggestion, made in the previous chapter, that God is indifferent to justice, and assures them that when God comes, preceded by his messenger, they will experience his judgment. This judgment is not seen by the prophet as mere destruction; it purifies and refines like fire.

*Philippians 4.4–9*
This passage continues the distinctive emphasis on joy found throughout this letter, and it is in this spirit that Paul commits the Phillippians to the peace of God. He then commends the accepted virtues of non-Christian society, but he also urges them to follow his own example and the Christian tradition they have received. It seems likely that even at this early stage there was a recognized summary of teaching common to Christian churches.

*Matthew 11.2–15*
Matthew records the enquiry that John the Baptist makes about Jesus. All the deeds that Jesus refers to in his answer have been recorded in the earlier chapters of the Gospel, so that the reader, as well as John the Baptist, is now invited to make up his own mind about the ministry of Jesus. Then Jesus speaks to the crowd about the Baptist, to whom he refers as 'Elijah', the forerunner of the kingdom.

## Second year, evening

*Amos 7.4–15*
The prophet Amos describes visions which reveal God's judgment on his people: one of fire, symbolizing destruction, and one of a plumb line, indicating the standard by which God tests the city and

finds it out of true. The prophet is reported to the king for his words
and told to prophesy elsewhere. Amos's reply shows that he does
not regard himself as a professional prophet, belonging to the court
of the king, but as a special prophet, directly under the orders of
God.

*Luke 3.1–17*
Luke introduces the ministry of John the Baptist, setting it in the
context of Roman and Jewish history, and quotes a prophecy of
Isaiah to show that John has come to prepare the people for the
judgment of God. Abraham cannot exempt them from that judgment; only repentance will save them, and that involves a radical
change in behaviour.


ASB
Prefaces as above.

# The Sunday before Christmas
(Advent 4)

---

*The Annunciation*

**First year, morning**

*Isaiah 11.1–9*

This prophecy speaks of the coming of a descendant of David, an ideal king who will possess the spirit of God. His reign will bring in a time of justice and peace, pictured here in poetic terms. Each time a future king was born in Israel, the people hoped for just such a ruler. They persisted in the belief that eventually a Messiah would come.

*1 Corinthians 1.26–31*

Paul invites the Christians at Corinth to take a realistic look at themselves. He reminds them that it is God's way to choose those whom the world despises. Paul's assertion that God is the source of all wisdom is intended to prevent the kind of boasting of which the Corinthians are in danger.

*Luke 1.26–38a*

Luke tells the story of the annunciation to Mary as a parallel to his story of the angel's visit to Zechariah, the father of John the Baptist. But, unlike John, Mary's child is described in language traditionally used of the Messiah. Luke attributes the conception of Jesus to the work of the Holy Spirit, and so introduces a theme which dominates his interpretation of the life of Jesus and his account of the early church.

**First year, evening**

*Isaiah 65.17–25*

Writing after the exile, the prophet speaks of the creation of a new heaven and a new earth. The new Jerusalem will be a place of joy, health, long life, freedom and communion with God. All this is a fulfilment of the picture in Chapter 11, painted by Isaiah of Jerusalem some 200 years before, but here there is no mention of a Messiah coming to bring in the new way of life.

*Luke 1.39–56*
Luke tells the story of Mary visiting Elizabeth, who is inspired to greet and acknowledge her with words that have become traditional in Catholic devotion. In the story, the unborn John the Baptist is already fulfilling his role of witnessing to Jesus. Mary responds with a hymn of praise, which is related to the song of Hannah in I Samuel and is full of references to the acts of God in Jewish history.

## Second year, morning

*Zechariah 2.10–13*
The prophet Zechariah not only speaks of God coming to be among the Jewish people, a common enough conviction among the prophets, but also enlarges the vision to include the hope that all nations will acknowledge God. The peoples of the world are therefore called to respond in awe to the coming of the Lord.

*Revelation 21.1–7*
The prophet unfolds a vision of God's intention of destroying evil and creating a new heaven and a new earth. Jerusalem will be transformed into the dwelling-place of God where he will be for ever with his people. Yet the vision is not primarily concerned with Jerusalem; it depicts God himself as the source and meaning of life for Christian people. 'He who conquers' is a reference to those who are being martyred for the faith.

*Matthew 1.18–23*
Matthew tells the story of the birth of Jesus as a fulfilment of Jewish scripture. The child about to be born is a sign of the presence of God, as both names testify: Jesus means 'one who saves', Emmanuel is translated as 'God with us'. The story is therefore not only about the birth of Jesus; it is also about the presence of God with his people.

## Second year, evening

*Jeremiah 23.5–8*
In a message of hope, Jeremiah proclaims that God will give to his people a truly righteous king. When he comes, God will deliver the people from exile as he once delivered their ancestors from Egypt

In language reminiscent of Isaiah of Jerusalem, the image of a branch from the family tree of David is used to express the hope of a deliverer.

*Revelation 22.6–17,20*
In this concluding passage of the book of Revelation, the author, a Christian prophet, makes his final witness to the truth of his message, claiming that God gave the revelation to Jesus, who has made it known to him through an angel. Because of the urgency of the message, the book is not to be sealed up but is to be issued at once. Clearly, the prophet expects the coming of Christ at any moment, and intends his writing to be a final preparation for it.

ASB
Prefaces as above.

**When this day is Christmas Eve, the evening lessons are:**

*Zechariah 2.10–13* See second year, morning. Or *Isaiah 11.1–9* See first year, morning.

*Titus 3.4–7*
The writer gives a summary of early Christian belief, taken perhaps from a service of baptism: the loving mercy of God has appeared in Jesus Christ; through baptism and the gift of the Spirit, Christians can receive God's gift of life.

ASB
**Christmas Eve: Years 1 and 2**

*Isaiah 62.1–5* See Fourth Sunday after Easter. First year, morning.

*Acts 13.16–26*
Paul is preaching in the Jewish synagogue at Pisidian Antioch in Asia Minor to both Jews and interested Gentiles. He expounds the meaning of the Jewish scripture as culminating in the coming of Jesus who is the fulfilment of God's promises.

## The Sunday before Christmas

*Luke 1.67–79*
Zechariah, the father of John the Baptist, greets his son's birth with a prophetic song, the *Benedictus*. This song draws upon passages from Jewish scripture, asserts that John is to be pre-eminent among the prophets and promises salvation to God's people.

# Christmas Day

*The Birth of Christ*

## First and second years, midnight

*Micah 5.2–4*
The prophet's message is that a Messiah will come out of Bethlehem, a place of little significance, and will restore Israel to greatness. This prophecy seems to belong to the years after the exile, when the people have returned to Jerusalem but are still awaiting a full restoration of their former greatness. The longing for a Messiah arises from the desire of the Jewish people to possess again the prosperity and blessings of the reign of David.

*Titus 2.11–15*
The writer reminds his readers of the purpose of the incarnation: God has appeared for the salvation of all men. This means that Christians must respond by living godly lives while awaiting the coming of the Lord. The incarnation and the expected return of Christ are thus closely linked by the writer: together they act as an encouragement to Christian living.

*Luke 2.1–20*
There are two emphases in this account of the birth of Jesus: he is the Jewish Messiah, born in Bethlehem in fulfilment of the ancient promises, and he is a saviour for the whole world, associated at his birth with events in the Roman empire. It is the shepherds, perhaps representing the poor, who first hear the news and acknowledge Jesus as saviour. In this way, a prominent theme of this Gospel, Jesus's special concern for the poor and their ready response to him, is anticipated.

## First and second years, morning

*Isaiah 9.2–7*
The prophet Isaiah celebrates what is either the birth or the day of enthronement of a king. He expresses the hope that this new king will fulfil the ideals that the people associate with the reign of David, so he is hailed with great ceremonial names. Although not a

prediction of Christ, the passage is treated in Christian tradition as a prophecy fulfilled in Jesus.

*I John 4.7–14*
The writer affirms that God is love. He knows this because he has seen God's love in Jesus Christ. This knowledge of God is the foundation of the writer's plea that Christians in his community should respond by loving one another, as God has loved them in Christ.

*John 1.1–14* See Ninth Sunday before Christmas. First year, morning.

## First year, evening

*Isaiah 60.13–22*
The prophet describes the new Jerusalem in language later used by the author of the book of Revelation. In this vision of the future, he speaks of the nations coming to the city of Jerusalem, which will be built with the finest materials and will express the divine glory on earth.

*Galatians 4.1–7*
Paul contrasts life under the law with the life of faith. Under the law man is a slave, subject to the demonic powers which, the ancient world thought, controlled the stars and the destinies of men. Paul believes that Christ has conquered these powers, and he is therefore able to describe the life of faith as freedom from them, and, more positively, as a life of sonship. The Spirit confirms this new relationship by enabling Christians, like Jesus, to address God as 'Father'.

## Second year, evening

*I Samuel 2.1–10*
This song of Hannah celebrates the triumph of the Israelites over their enemies and praises God who controls the fortunes of his people. Under God, the dispossessed can inherit the earth. The song is later used as the basis of the *Magnificat,* and affirms that God will give strength to his anointed one. It is very much like a royal psalm in character, hailing the anointed king in language used also of the Messiah.

*Philippians 2.5–11*
Paul invites the Christians at Philippi to cultivate within their fellowship a quality of life based on communion with Christ. He therefore recalls the example of Christ, particularly his humility and self-denial for the sake of others. The passage is thought to be an early Christian hymn on the theme of the humiliation and exaltation of Christ.


# ASB
## Years 1 and 2

*Isaiah 9.2,6–7*   See Preface for Isaiah 9.2–7, as above.

*Isaiah 62.10–12*
The prophet addresses pilgrims returning to the city of Jerusalem to worship there at the end of the exile. The proclamation is one of deliverance and salvation.

*Micah 5.2–4*   Preface as above.

*Titus 2.11–14; 3.3–7*   See Preface for Titus 2.11–15 as above.

*Hebrews 1.1–5*   See The Sunday after Christmas, First year, morning.

*1 John 4.7–14*   Preface as above.

*Luke 2.1–14 (15–20)* or *Luke 2.8–20*   See Preface for Luke 2.1–20 as above.

*John 1.1–14*   Preface as above.

# The Sunday after Christmas

*The Wise Men*

**First year, morning**

*Isaiah 60.1–6*
The prophet, speaking at a time when some of the Jews have
returned from exile to Jerusalem and the temple has been rebuilt,
gives a picture of the new Jerusalem for which he longs. His vision
is that all the nations of the world will come to the holy city, bringing
their riches. Then Jerusalem will prosper and its glory will be known,
as in the time of Solomon.

*Hebrews 1.1–4*
This letter opens with a description of how God's plan is fulfilled in
Christ. At first God spoke through the prophets, but now he speaks
through his Son. The finality of Christ's work is stressed. He is now
enthroned in glory, evidence of the perfect sacrifice he has made.

*Matthew 2.1–12*
Matthew tells the story of the wise men coming to Bethlehem. There
is a great contrast between the way the wise men and king Herod
react to the same news: one with joy and gifts, the other with fear
and slaughter. The wise men in the story are Gentiles and symbolize
the faith that Christ is Lord of the whole world.

**First year, evening**

*Isaiah 49.13–23*
The prophet has spoken of Israel's role as a light to the nations. But
he knows that he is addressing a nation at present humiliated, and
he answers the complaint of this forgotten people by using images of
God's constant love. In her exile, Israel may feel barren, widowed
and divorced, but God promises restoration for his people.

*I John 1.1–2.2*
In a situation of conflict and division, the writer looks back to the
historical events of the life of Jesus and reminds his readers of the
fellowship that Christians have with God and Christ. He wishes to

convince his people that forgiveness is available if they confess their sin and receive the gift of new life. Christ is called an 'advocate', the one who can speak on behalf of Christians to the Father; and, in thought and language drawn from Jewish religion, he is also described as the 'expiation' or sacrificial offering for sin: the one who wins God over to their side.

## Second year, morning

*Isaiah 49.7–13*
The prophet has already announced God's plan for the restoration of Israel. He now presents God's purpose, to be achieved through those who are suffering humiliation in exile. The return from Babylon is not to be the end of God's hopes for Israel, for she has a mission to other nations, indeed to the whole world.

*Ephesians 3.1–6*
The writer of this letter describes how Jews and Gentiles have come together in the Christian church because Christ has made peace between them. This is God's secret plan, a mystery now revealed to his apostles and prophets.

*Matthew 2.1–12*   See Sunday after Christmas. First year, morning.

## Second year, evening

*Isaiah 61.1–11*
Speaking to a rather disappointed people, the prophet unfolds with vigour a picture of restoration and encourages them to see new possibilities in the homeland to which they have returned from exile. The basis of this great hope is the promise of God's blessing and the renewal of his covenant relationship with them.

*Romans 15.13–21*
Paul here writes in a personal way about his ministry. He knows the importance of the Christian community at Rome and feels the need to affirm the source of his authority to a people he has not yet visited. At the centre of all his thought and activity is his call to be a minister of Christ to the Gentiles.

*The Sunday after Christmas*

ASB
**Year 1**

*Isaiah 7.10–14*
God promises king Ahaz a sign to confirm the truth of Isaiah's advice to him at a time when the enemy is at the city gate. The sign is the birth of a royal son, a continuance of the dynasty, whose name is a promise of God's presence with his people.

*Galatians 4.1–7*   See Christmas Day. First year, evening.

*John 1.14–18*
The concluding words of the prologue of John's Gospel speak of the incarnation of Jesus Christ as the revelation of God's glory. As such it is a promise of God's grace and truth.

**Year 2**

See Second Sunday after Christmas. First year, morning.

# Second Sunday after Christmas

## *The Presentation in the Temple*

### First year, morning

*1 Samuel 1.20–28*
Hannah, deeply sorrowful that she is childless, has vowed that, if she has a son, she will dedicate him to God. Now that a child has been born, she takes him to the temple at Shiloh, with the customary offerings, and leaves him there in Eli's care to be trained as a priest. Shiloh, an important sanctuary at this time, was the place where the Ark was kept.

*Romans 12.1–8*
Paul introduces this chapter dealing with Christian behaviour with a statement that the foundation of Christian conduct is surrender to God. He uses the language of sacrifice to make his point. This new life is to be lived within the church, where God's gifts are to be used for the benefit of other Christians.

*Luke 2.21–40*
Luke tells the story of Jesus's circumcision and presentation in the temple. The account is reminiscent of the dedication of Samuel, and so presents Jesus as a great prophet. But the song of Simeon leads to a greater claim: Jesus is to be a light to the Gentiles. This judgment is confirmed by the prophetess Anna, who also recognizes in Jesus the fulfilment of the hopes of the Jewish people.

### First year, evening

*Isaiah 40.25–31*
The prophet assures the exiled people of God's power to restore them. He speaks of the incomparable nature of God. This nature is illustrated by reference to the creation: God who has power to create is able to give strength and renewal to his people. It is their calling to wait expectantly for him.

*Colossians 1.1–14*
Paul writes with greetings and thanksgiving to the Christians at Colossae, commending them for their wisdom and understanding

and hoping that they will continue to grow in the Christian life. He is anxious that they should not underestimate what Christ has done, and therefore reminds them of the gospel he preaches. God is the source of their new life; he has brought them from the rule of darkness to the kingdom of Christ.

## *The Visit to Jerusalem*

### Second year, morning

*Deuteronomy 16.1–6*
The Israelites are urged to keep the feast of the Passover each year. This feast, celebrated in the spring, probably began as a sacrifice of the first-born animals, but was later interpreted, as in this passage, as a commemoration of the deliverance of the Israelites from Egypt. The unleavened bread is a symbolic reminder of the days of affliction in Egypt and of the night of the Hebrews' escape.

*Romans 8.12–17*
Paul uses the word 'flesh' to refer not exclusively to the physical, but to the whole of human nature when in opposition to God. He urges Christians to live the new life under the Spirit, and speaks of its chief characteristic, the gift of sonship. In using this image, Paul has drawn upon both the Roman law of adoption, which meant coming under the authority of a new father, and the Jewish law of adoption, with its emphasis on becoming an heir. Paul, like Jesus, uses the Aramaic word 'Abba', an intimate term for 'father'.

*Luke 2.41–52*
In a story reminiscent of the boyhood of Samuel, Luke tells of a visit to Jerusalem by Jesus and his parents. This visit celebrates the time when Jesus is able to accept for himself the obligations to which his parents had committed him at his circumcision. The story contrasts the responsibility Jesus feels towards his parents with that which he has to God, and so emphasizes his growing awareness of his special relationship with God.

### Second year, evening

*Haggai 2.1–9*
The prophet Haggai has an encouraging message for those who are reconstructing the temple in Jerusalem after the exile. Their building

may not be as great as the previous temple, but God is there with them. Then follows a vision of the last age in which the nations pay tribute to God in Jerusalem. In that day the temple will be an even more splendid place than before.

*Luke 2.21–40*   See Second Sunday after Christmas. First year, morning.

# ASB
## Year 1

*Ecclesiasticus 3.2–7*
The author of this piece of Hebrew wisdom believes that virtue will be rewarded. He therefore urges respect and obedience to parents as both a service to God and a sure means of future happiness.

*Exodus 12.21–27*
This passage contains one of the accounts of the institution of the feast of the Passover, a feast which is to be observed in the promised land as a reminder of God's deliverance. This account places great stress on the use of blood to protect the Israelite homes from the destruction of the first-born.

*Romans 8.11–17*   Preface as above.

*Luke 2.41 – end*   Preface as above.

## Year 2

See Epiphany. Second year.

# Epiphany

## First year

*Isaiah 49.1–13*
The prophet speaks about the role of the 'servant', that is, the nation Israel, or at least its faithful members. He declares that the restored Israel will have a mission to be God's witness to other nations, indeed to the whole world.

*Ephesians 3.1–12* See Sunday after Christmas. Second year, morning.

*Matthew 2.1–20* See Sunday after Christmas. First year, morning. Preface for Matthew 2.1–12.

## Second year

*Isaiah 60.1–6* See Sunday after Christmas. First year, morning.

*Revelation 21.22–22.5*
This passage is part of the prophet's vision of a new heaven and a new earth. He sees a city without a temple, but blessed for ever with the presence of God. He also sees a river and a tree, symbols of life, in the heavenly city where God will always reign.

*Matthew 2.1–20* See Sunday after Christmas. First year, morning. Preface for Matthew 2.1–12.

## ASB
## Years 1 and 2

*Isaiah 49.1–6* See Preface for Isaiah 49.1–13 as above.

*Ephesians 3.1–12* Preface as above.

*Matthew 2.1–12* See Sunday after Christmas. First year, morning.

# First Sunday after Epiphany

*The Baptism of Christ*

### First year, morning

*I Samuel 16.1–13a*
The story of the anointing of David is used by the writer to link the leadership of David with that of Samuel. Both men are chosen by God. Other stories in the book suggest that David comes to power through his own abilities, but this account puts the emphasis on God's choice of David, symbolized most clearly by God's spirit coming upon him. This is not just a general sign of God's favour, but is traditionally associated in Jewish scripture with prophets and kings.

*Acts 10.34–48a*
The writer has recounted how Peter received a vision which prepared him to go to the Gentile house of the centurion Cornelius to preach the gospel. Now he records Peter's speech there: it is a brief summary of the ministry of Jesus, prefaced by an assurance that God is willing to receive devout Gentiles. The story concludes with an account of the Gentiles receiving the Holy Spirit and being baptized.

*Matthew 3.13–17*
Matthew tells the story of the baptism of Christ. After the baptism, the Spirit comes on Jesus as a dove, the symbol of Israel, and a voice speaks from heaven. The symbolism of the dove and the voice suggest that Jesus is the one chosen to lead a new Israel and that the last age of history has begun.

### First year, evening

*Exodus 14.5–18*
This, the story of the flight of the Israelites from Egypt, tells of the Egyptian decision to pursue them and of the way of escape provided by God. The story attributes everything that happens to the action of God. There is a great contrast between the doubting reaction of the people of Israel and the certainty of Moses that God will support them.

*First Sunday after Epiphany*

*Mark 1.1–11*
Mark's Gospel opens with an acknowledgment that Jesus is the Son
of God, a claim confirmed by the words symbolically spoken at his
baptism. The ministry of Jesus is introduced by John the Baptist,
the announcer of the Messiah, whose work is to prepare for the
ministry of Jesus. The whole passage serves as a prologue to the
gospel story in which the identity of Jesus is confirmed for the reader.

## Second year, morning

*Isaiah 42.1–7*
The prophet speaks of the task of the servant, who receives God's
spirit in order to administer justice among the nations. In this role,
Israel will fulfil her covenant vow and be of continuing service to the
Gentile nations.

*Ephesians 2.1–10*
The writer contrasts the state of the Ephesian Christians before their
baptism with the life to which they are now called. He stresses that
it is only through the work of God's grace that Christians are released
from the powers of evil and are living a new life in Christ. The
passage contains a clear summary of Paul's teaching on salvation,
emphasizing what is brought about by God's grace.

*John 1.29–34*
The writer of John's Gospel records the baptism of Jesus as part of
the testimony of John the Baptist, who fulfils the role, assigned to
him in the prologue, of witnessing to Christ. He refers to Jesus as
the lamb of God, recalling the Passover lamb sacrificed at the annual
festival, and preparing the reader for the account of the death of
Jesus at the time when the Passover lamb was slain. The writer
confirms that Jesus is the promised Jewish Messiah, and makes it
clear that the Spirit of God has come upon him.

## Second year, evening

*Joshua 3.1–17*
This is the story of the crossing of the river Jordan by the Israelites
under Joshua's leadership. The ark, a wooden box in which the two
stone tablets of the law were kept, plays an important part in this

*40*

,tory, and the distance the people have to keep from it indicates its 1oliness. The story witnesses to the power of God and his protection )f the Israelites, who are enabled to enter the promised land only hrough what they see as God's miraculous help.

*Romans 6.12–23*

'aul has already explained that the consequence of dying with Christ n baptism is resurrection to a new life. Now he draws out the )ractical implication of this belief. Christians live under grace, which neans not freedom to sin but obedience to God.

\SB

'refaces as above.

# Second Sunday after Epiphany

## The First Disciples

### First year, morning

*Jeremiah 1.4–10*
Jeremiah relates his call from God to be a prophet. The accoun
witnesses to an intense inner experience and reveals Jeremiah'
deeply personal relationship with God. This call comes to be the ke
influence in the prophet's later ministry, providing him with a poin
of stability and power in an otherwise troubled and vulnerable life

*Acts 26.1,9–18*
The writer gives an account of Paul's defence before king Agripp
at Caesarea. Paul speaks of his experience on the road to Damascu
and of the call he received there to be a minister to the Gentiles
This acccunt compares Paul's ministry to that of the servant i
Isaiah, because that is the part of Jewish scripture where th
conversion of the Gentiles is most clearly announced.

*Mark 1.14–20*
Mark gives a summary of the preaching of Jesus, suggesting that th
end of time and the rule of God are present in his ministry. It is i
this context that Mark records the call of the first disciples, whos
immediate response is to follow Jesus. Mark seeks to evoke the sam
reaction from his readers.

### First year, evening

*Ezekiel 2.1–3.3*
In a vision, Ezekiel has been confronted by the majesty of God an
now God calls him to be his prophet. Because the message c
judgment is unpalatable and the people are likely to reject it, th
prophet is made to eat the scroll containing it. This symbolic ac
prevents Ezekiel from avoiding the task committed to him.

*Matthew 10.1–15*
Matthew records the call of the disciples, their names and th
authority Jesus gives to them. They are sent to Jews only, and th

message they preach is identical with that of Jesus himself: the kingdom is near. Matthew sees the ministry of Jesus as confined almost entirely to Jews until after his resurrection, when the disciples are commissioned to preach to all nations.


## Second year, morning

*1 Samuel 3.1–10*
The young Samuel, dedicated to God by his mother, serves Eli in the temple. Spending the night in the sanctuary, he receives the call of God to be a prophet. Soon he is recognized throughout all Israel as a prophet and as the leader of the people, especially in their conflict with the Philistines.

*Galatians 1.11–24*
In an autobiographical passage, Paul speaks heatedly to the Galatians about the origin and truth of his gospel and his relationship with the church at Jerusalem. His aim is to show that his commission to be an apostle to the Gentiles was received directly from Christ and was not dependent upon the authority of the Jerusalem church.

*John 1.35–51*
The writer of John's Gospel tells how the first disciples come to follow Jesus in response to the testimony of their leader, John the Baptist, and how they, in turn, are responsible for the calling of others. This account contrasts with the other Gospels, where Jesus himself takes the initiative. Built into this story is a belief in Jesus as Messiah, fulfiller of the Jewish scriptures, king of Israel and the unique mediator between heaven and earth.


## Second year, evening

*1 Kings 18.21–39*
This passage recounts how the people are made to choose between Yahweh, the God of Israel, and Baal, the Canaanite god. According to the story, a contest is arranged by Elijah on Mount Carmel, a place sacred to both religions. Yahweh is shown to be effective in his authority over the elements, and the people respond by acknowledging him as lord. The story contrasts the clear, decisive action of Elijah with the ineffectual ravings of the prophets of Baal. It has a

brutal ending in the following verse: for the sake of Yahweh the prophets of Baal are slaughtered.

### Acts 9.1–20

This is the first account in Acts of the conversion of Saul. The appearance of Jesus himself lies at the heart of the story, though it is not until Ananias goes to Saul that the conversion is complete and he is baptized Paul. The contrast is strongly made between Saul the persecutor of Jesus and Paul the preacher, proclaiming that Jesus is the Son of God. The story is not just one of conversion, for the writer uses it to indicate the commission which God gives to Paul to preach to the Gentiles.


### ASB
Prefaces as above.

# Third Sunday after Epiphany

*The First Sign: The Wedding at Cana*

**First year, morning**

*Exodus 33.12–23*
Moses is assured of God's favour, but wants to know how other people are to be convinced of this. He is therefore promised admission into God's presence. But the full glory of God is too mysterious to be comprehended and too radiant to be seen, so Moses is allowed to see what is symbolically called 'the back of God'.

*I John 1.1–4*
In a situation of conflict and division, the writer looks back to the foundations of his community's life: the historical events of the life of Jesus and the experience of fellowship with him and with the Father.

*John 2.1–11*
The writer of John's Gospel describes the turning of water into wine as the first sign that Jesus performed. 'Sign' is the writer's characteristic word for miracles attributed to Jesus, and is used of acts which point to the meaning of his ministry and reveal his glory. The 'hour' of Jesus is the hour of glory on the cross. The jars of water for the Jewish rites of purification represent the old covenant, now superseded by the greater glory of the new covenant, symbolized by the wine.

**First year, evening**

*Numbers 9.15–23*
During their time in the wilderness, the Israelites keep the tabernacle, which houses the ark of the covenant, in the middle of their camp. Cloud over the tabernacle during the day and fire at night are to them the signs of God's presence; only when the cloud lifts do they move on. The story witnesses to the belief that all the activity of the Israelites is at the express command of God, and that they are assured of his presence with them continually.

*Third Sunday after Epiphany*

*Mark 1.21–34*
Mark has gathered together material which testifies to the healing ministry of Jesus. By placing such material at the beginning of the Gospel, he witnesses to the power of God at work in Jesus, and confirms to his readers the claim he has already made that Jesus is the Son of God. The authority of Jesus, as both teacher and healer, is therefore quickly established.

## The New Temple

### Second year, morning

*I Kings 8.22–30*
This is the account of Solomon's prayer at the dedication of the temple in Jerusalem, which he has built in fulfilment of God's promise to David. The ark has been brought to Jerusalem for the autumn festival and placed in the inner shrine of the temple, an action which symbolizes the mysterious presence of God dwelling among men. Solomon prays that the temple will be a place where God will hear the prayers of his people.

*I Corinthians 3.10–17*
Paul writes to the Corinthian Christians about the influence other leaders are having on them. In the case of those who contend for Jewish exclusiveness, the fire of judgment will destroy the false building they are erecting. In this analogy of the church as a building, Paul stresses that the foundation is Jesus Christ himself, a metaphor which leads him to speak of the Christian community as the temple where God's Spirit dwells. Here Paul has a concern both for the purity of the Corinthian community and for the recognition of his own apostleship among them.

*John 2.13–22*
The writer of John's Gospel places the cleansing of the temple at the opening of the ministry of Jesus. When his authority is challenged, Jesus causes consternation by speaking of the destruction and rebuilding of the temple, interpreted here as the destruction of his own body, the place where God's Spirit dwells. The writer stresses that it will only be after the resurrection that the meaning of Jesus's words will become clear to the disciples.

**Second year, evening**

*Numbers 21.4–9*
From a number of incidents, it is clear that the people of Israel find
the freedom of the desert too much for them and long for the security
of their old slavery. When they grumble at the way they are being
led by Moses, they are punished with a plague of serpents. Moses is
enabled to re-establish his authority through the immunity granted
to those who look upon the bronze serpent. The story has a strong
element of superstition, but it witnesses to the sovereignty of God
and the leadership of Moses.

*John 3.1–15*
Nicodemus, a leading Jew, comes to Jesus seeking the kingdom of
God. When Jesus says he must be born anew, Nicodemus fails to
understand that he means a renewal of human life by God's Spirit,
as later expressed in baptism. In this story, the writer treats Nicodemus as a representative of the Jews, and so the conversation is
presented as part of the debate between the church and Judaism. As
salvation came to those who looked at the image of the serpent in
the wilderness, so Christians gaze on the Son of man, lifted up in
glory on the cross, and receive eternal life.

ASB
**Year 1**

*Exodus 33.12 – end*   Preface as above.

*I John 1.1–7*
In a situation of conflict and division, the writer looks back to the
foundations of his community's life: the historical events of the life
of Jesus and the experience of fellowship with him and with the
Father. Christians are called to live in God's light and in fellowship
with one another.

*John 2.1–11*   Preface as above.

**Year 2**

See Seventh Sunday before Easter. First year, morning.

# Fourth Sunday after Epiphany

## The Friend of Sinners

### First year, morning

*Hosea 14.1–7*
The first part of this passage is an expression of repentance on behalf of the nation. The second part is God's response: he will forgive the people and restore them to life and prosperity. The disaster brought on Israel by her sin will be reversed through her repentance. The people are therefore called upon to make confession of sin and receive forgiveness.

*Philemon 1–16*
Paul writes to Philemon about Onesimus, a slave, who has run away from Philemon and come to see Paul in prison. Paul has developed some affection for Onesimus, perhaps bringing him to the Christian faith. Now he sends him back as a Christian brother and clearly hopes that Philemon will release him, so that he can be of wider Christian service.

*Mark 2.13–17*
Mark uses the call of Levi to introduce the conflict that has arisen over the way Jesus makes friends with tax collectors and sinners. 'Sinners' here means the ordinary people who do not observe the law as strictly interpreted by the Pharisees. By eating with them, Jesus offends strict Jews, just as, later, Jewish Christians who ate with Gentiles offended their stricter brethren. Jesus neither condemns nor condones sinners; he calls them to repentance.

### First year, evening

*Genesis 32.3–12*
This story tells of Jacob's return to Canaan with sufficient wealth and power to secure peace with his brother Esau, whom he has wronged. Despite this security, he is afraid of meeting Esau, and so he sends gifts ahead to appease him and divides his flock in case of attack. He then prays to God for deliverance. This prayer describes Jacob's relationship with God in very personal terms, a feature

vividly portrayed in the account of Jacob wrestling with God which follows this passage. The story has a happy ending, for the two brothers are reconciled.

*I Timothy 1.12–17*
The writer of this letter to Timothy describes himself as a persecutor who has turned into God's servant. This experience, which witnesses to the mercy and grace of God, leads him to affirm the doctrine, so central to this letter, that Christ came into the world to save sinners. The passage is clearly a comment on the life and experience of Paul.


*Life for the World*

**Second year, morning**

*I Kings 10.1–13*
This is the story of the queen of Sheba's visit to the court of king Solomon in Jerusalem. The queen probably ruled in northern Arabia, and seems to have come to Jerusalem mainly to develop trading links with Israel. Possibly she came also to pay homage to Solomon, a powerful neighbouring ruler, and to ensure peace between them. The writer interprets Solomon's wealth and the splendour of his court as a sign of God's blessing.

*Ephesians 3.8–19*
The writer reminds his mainly Gentile readers that he has been called to be an apostle to the Gentiles as part of God's plan that the whole world should be saved. His prayer for them is that they should have fellowship with Christ and know his love.

*John 4.7–14*
The writer of John's Gospel has described how Jesus passes through Samaria and sits down at a well where he meets a Samaritan woman. Jesus, though physically thirsty and dependent on the Samaritan woman for water, is able to offer her 'water that gives eternal life', that is, the knowledge of God and of himself. The story shows how Jesus fulfils the hopes of the Samaritans, just as he fulfils the hopes of the Jews.

*Fourth Sunday after Epiphany*

## Second year, evening

*Zechariah 8.1–8, 20–23*
In this collection of prophetic sayings from the period after the return of the Jews from exile, Zechariah paints a picture of the age of salvation when God's promises will be fulfilled and Jerusalem will be a blessed and holy city. The promises include safety in its streets and the return of the scattered Jews from all over the earth. The vision of non-Jews coming to Jerusalem to acknowledge God reflects the developing belief that God is lord of all nations.

*I John 5.1–12*
The writer affirms that belief in the incarnation enables the Christian to enter the family of God and overcome the evil of the world. Symbolically, through reference to the water and the blood, he affirms the reality of Christ's baptism and death, and reflects the practice of baptism and the Lord's Supper in the life of the early church. The Spirit also is said to be a witness to the incarnation.

## ASB
## Year 1

See Third Sunday after Epiphany. Second year, morning.

## Year 2

*Jeremiah 7.1–11*  See Seventeenth Sunday after Pentecost. First year, morning.

*Hebrews 12.18 – end*
The writer recalls the experience of the Israelites at Mount Sinai, and contrasts their covenant with the new covenant made in Christ. At Mount Sinai, the people experienced dread; at Mount Zion, the new Jerusalem, they experience God's grace. 'The blood of Abel' refers to Genesis 4.10. Abel's blood called for vengeance on Cain; Christ's blood calls for reconciliation. The passage concludes with a solemn warning and the assurance of an unshakeable kingdom.

*John 4.19–26*  See Sixth Sunday after Epiphany. Second year, morning.

# Fifth Sunday after Epiphany

*The New Dispensation*

### First year, morning

*Joel 2.15–19, 21–22*
The prophet Joel reacts to a severe plague of locusts by summoning the people to fasting and repentance and by asking the priests to organize a national day of prayer. The prophet fears not only the disaster the locusts can bring, but also the reaction of the surrounding nations, who will wonder what has happened to Israel's God. But, in response to their repentance, the prophet assures the people of God's forgiveness and blessing, and promises a plentiful harvest.

*II Corinthians 3.4–11*
Paul explains that his confidence is not based on his own sufficiency but on God. He then contrasts the killing effect of the old Jewish law with the new life of the Spirit.

*Mark 2.18–22*
Jesus is asked why his disciples do not fast. He justifies their behaviour by using the imagery of the bridegroom, suggesting that, as the kingdom of God is present, it is not a proper time to fast. The point is reinforced by further illustrations which show that, in the ministry of Jesus, God is at work in a new way.

### First year, evening

*I Kings 21.1–19*
This is the story of the way in which king Ahab gains Naboth's vineyard. By refusing to sell his vineyard, part of his family inheritance, Naboth acts according to Israelite tradition. Queen Jezebel, a non-Israelite, arranges for the death of Naboth and so enables Ahab to seize the property. Elijah's intervention illustrates the continuing conflict between the king and the prophet of God.

*John 3.22–36*
The writer of John's Gospel describes how John the Baptist testifies to the identity of Jesus and refuses to see him as a rival. There may

have been those in the early church who gave an excessive devotion to John the Baptist, which the author of this Gospel wishes to discourage. The story contains the only claim in the New Testament that Jesus himself baptized.

## Work

### Second year, morning

*Lamentations 3.19–26*
This passage reflects the despair felt by those left in Judah after the destruction of Jerusalem and the removal of most of the Jews to exile. But in the midst of bitterness, the writer seeks to remind his readers that there is a true source of hope: God's unceasing love.

*I Thessalonians 5.12–24*
Paul concludes his letter to the church at Thessalonica with advice on the life of the Christian community. Leaders of the congregation are to be respected and the highest standards of community life are to be upheld.

*Matthew 20.1–15*
Matthew records the parable of the labourers in the vineyard, in which an unusual feature emerges: everyone is paid the same wage regardless of the hours worked. The parable suggests that God's treatment of penitent men and women will be without discrimination. Such treatment is illustrated in the ministry of Jesus.

### Second year, evening

*Zechariah 10.6–12*
In a passage which is in the form of a direct address by God, the prophet speaks of a new hope for the people and of a return from exile. The imagery of crossing the sea is reminiscent of the release of the Israelites from Egypt and their entry into the promised land. The picture is therefore one of restoration through a new exodus and the beginning of a golden age.

*James 5.7–11*
James advises patience at a time when the coming of the Lord is thought to be imminent. In a manner typical of Jewish argument, he

gives a number of illustrations. These suggest that, whereas some Christians will simply have to be patient, others will have their endurance tested by suffering and persecution.

## ASB
## Years 1 and 2

*Proverbs 2.1–9*
The writer urges the pursuit of wisdom as a great treasure, leading to the knowledge of God himself. Such wisdom is God's gift to men.

*Ecclesiasticus 42.15 – end*
The writer expresses his belief in God's complete sovereignty over all creation. This passage is in effect a hymn in praise of God as creator and sustainer of life, the one who gives meaning to all that is.

*I Corinthians 3.18 – end*   See Sixth Sunday after Epiphany. First year, morning.

*Matthew 12.38–42*
In response to the demand for a sign to support his teaching, Jesus refers to the prophet Jonah: Matthew interprets the sign of Jonah's deliverance from the great fish as prefiguring the resurrection and he laments the failure of the Jews to believe the sign.

# Sixth Sunday after Epiphany

*The Right Use of the Sabbath*

## First year, morning

*Isaiah 1.10–17*
Early in his ministry, perhaps on a feast day, the prophet Isaiah speaks about the worthlessness of mere ritual. This is a familiar and powerful prophetic message: sacrifice, no matter how lavish, is worthless unless accompanied by righteousness. It is not the temple worship, as such, that is being attacked, but rather its separation from everyday conduct.

*I Corinthians 3.18–23*
Paul here attacks those leaders at Corinth who present themselves as wise, and quotes Job and the Psalms against their claim to wisdom. He reminds the Corinthian Christians that they do not belong to the one who converted them, but only to Christ.

*Mark 2.23–3.6*
Mark relates two incidents that happen on a Sabbath day: the disciples of Jesus pluck ears of corn and Jesus himself heals a man with a withered hand. In both cases, Jesus is challenged about Sabbath observance, and confounds his critics with a counter-question. The stories witness both to the growing opposition to Jesus in the course of his ministry and to the continuing concern of the early church about the observance by Christians of the Jewish Sabbath.

## First year, evening

*Genesis 18.20–33*
In this story Abraham is admitted to God's inner counsels and allowed to plead for the sinful people of Sodom. His chief interest in the safety of the city is that his nephew Lot lives there. Abraham's appeal to God's justice is successful but, according to a later story, though Lot is saved, the city of Sodom is destroyed, for not even ten righteous people could be found in it.

*Luke 13.1–9*

The occasion of these sayings is the news that some Galileans have been killed in the temple. Luke shows how Jesus uses this, and another disastrous incident, to refute the notion that calamity is the inevitable result of sin. At the same time he emphasizes the need for repentance. Jesus reinforces the message with a parable, which is probably to be understood as the offer of a last chance to Israel.

# The Holy Mountain

## Second year, morning

*Exodus 19.16–24*

In this story the Israelites are encamped at Sinai, where Moses prepares them to meet with God. The first sign is thick cloud, symbolizing the mystery of God. Then follow volcanic smoke and fire, symbolizing the awe-inspiring presence of the divine. The incident takes place immediately before the giving of the ten commandments.

*Hebrews 12.18 – 29*

The writer of the letter to the Hebrews recalls the experience of the Israelites at Mount Sinai, and contrasts their covenant with the new covenant made in Christ. The new covenant is superior to the old, and it is therefore more perilous than before to ignore the voice of God. At the day of judgment, only the unshakeable things will survive: chief among them, the kingdom established through Christ.

*John 4.19–26*

In this passage, the writer of John's Gospel continues his account of the conversation between Jesus and the Samaritan woman. They refer to the places where Samaritans and Jews worship: Mount Gerizim and Jerusalem. Out of this conversation emerges both the writer's understanding of God as Father and his claim that Jesus is the expected Messiah.

## Second year, evening

*1 Kings 5.19b–27*

Following the healing of Naaman in the waters of the Jordan, Gehazi, Elisha's servant, seizes the opportunity to gain wealth for himself. Elisha, however, is aware of his action and transfers Naaman's leprosy to him: a punishment for his opportunism. The story illustrates both the belief in the supernatural power of the prophet and the severity with which he rejects deceitful and dishonest behaviour.

*Matthew 22.1–14*
Matthew records the parable of the wedding feast, a story containing a strong note of judgment, with the Jews particularly in mind. The burning of the city perhaps reflects the destruction of Jerusalem in AD 70. In the second part of the parable, the man who has no wedding garment is cast out: a warning to Christians that they too will be rejected if they do not wear the garments of good and right behaviour.


## ASB
**Years 1 and 2**

*II Samuel 12.1 – 10*
   See Ninth Sunday before Easter. First year, evening.

*Romans 1.18–25*
Paul speaks of all mankind being exposed to the influence of evil and thus coming under the retribution of God. He refers particularly to the Gentiles and their practice of idolatry. They have ignored the signs of the Creator, discernible by reason, and instead have worshipped the objects of his creation.

*Matthew 13.24–30*
This parable warns against a premature attempt to distinguish between those people who have responded to God's kingdom and those who have not.

# Ninth Sunday before Easter

*Christ the Teacher*

**First year, morning**

*Isaiah 30.18–21*
God is here depicted as the Teacher of Israel who has led his people through difficult times and will show them the way ahead. The reference to seeing and hearing the Teacher cannot be meant literally, if the Teacher is God, and probably refers to the revelation of God through the teachers of the law.

*1 Corinthians 4.8–13*
Paul seeks to defend his ministry to those at Corinth who despise it, and he ridicules the self-importance of his opponents. He strongly contrasts the position of the apostles, among whom he numbers himself, with the Corinthians, who think too highly of themselves. A true apostle, he argues, is a rejected person, held in little esteem.

*Matthew 5.1–12*
The sermon on the mount, the first of five collections of teaching in Matthew's Gospel, opens with the beatitudes. They provide a summary of the teaching of Jesus marked by a strong moral tone. Each beatitude opens in the well-known Jewish form 'Blessed are . .', and the teaching is presented in a way similar to that found in the book of Proverbs.

**First year, evening**

*2 Samuel 12.1–14*
Following the death of Uriah, arranged by David so that he could have Uriah's wife for himself, Nathan the prophet comes to David and accuses him in the name of the Lord. Nathan then delivers God's judgment on David. It is a harsh one. The story illustrates vividly the relationship between prophet and king, and the fearless way in which the prophets spoke in the name of the Lord.

*Mark 4.21–34*
In this series of parables and sayings, Jesus illustrates the nature of the kingdom of God, using images from everyday life. According to

this account, the people do not understand what Jesus is saying and he has to explain the parables to his disciples. This may be a device used by Mark to show why Jesus was not generally recognized as the Messiah, but it also reflects a genuine feature of parables, that only those who are willing to listen to them and think about them will grasp their point.

## Second year, morning

*Proverbs 3.1–8*
This passage urges the reader to obey the teachings of God as contained in the law, and to observe them inwardly and not merely in outward appearance. The reward for obedience to God's ways is said to be peace and long life. This was the general Hebrew view, reflected in much of the Old Testament, though challenged by the book of Job and rejected by the preacher in Ecclesiastes.

*I Corinthians 2.1–10*
Paul has been contrasting human rhetoric and wisdom with God's wisdom, and has argued that God has chosen the weak and foolish to preach the gospel. It is in this context that he wants the Corinthians to understand his own ministry and the nature of his preaching: he wishes to impart God's wisdom, not man's. Jewish wisdom literature had already spoken of divine wisdom and Paul identifies this wisdom with Jesus Christ.

*Luke 8.4–15*
In the parable of the sower, Jesus refers to an everyday event, but into it an unexpected note is introduced which catches the attention of the listener: the amazing yield from the good soil. There follows a reference to parables not being understood. This may be a means of explaining why Jesus was not generally recognized as Messiah, but it also reflects the fact that the meaning of parables does not usually lie on the surface. Luke then uses this parable to encourage preachers to persevere in their teaching and Christian disciples to be faithful to what they have been taught.

## Second year, evening

*Job 28.12–28*
This passage about the source of wisdom and man's search for it appears to be a separate poem inserted into the book of Job. The

quest for wisdom – the finer values of life – is shown to be different from the pursuit of material riches. No search on earth will reveal the source of wisdom, for it is a spiritual quality whose origin lies with God himself. It can only be discovered through the worship and reverence of God: this is the 'fear of the Lord'.

*Matthew 13.44–58*
In the first two parables, the kingdom of God is compared to treasure and fine pearls for which men search. In the third, Matthew introduces, in current terms, the note of judgment. He concludes the collection of parables with a stress on the understanding or wisdom required for their message to be received. The wise disciple, in his search for the kingdom, will be able to draw on both the teaching of Jesus and the teaching of the church. In the concluding verses, the reaction of the people to the teaching of Jesus in his home synagogue confirms the suggestion already made by Matthew, that Jesus is the source of wisdom.

# ASB
Prefaces as above.

# Eighth Sunday before Easter

*Christ the Healer*

### First year, morning

*Zephaniah 3.14–20*
The book of Zephaniah closes with a prediction of what the golden age will be like for Israel. Her enemies will be defeated, the scattered Jews will return to Jerusalem and there will be general joy at the restoration of God's people. The tone of the passage is unlike that of the early part of the book and seems to reflect a later period after the exile, when there was a new mood of hope.

*James 5.13–16*
James commends the power of prayer, especially when anyone is ill. He suggests that the elders of the church should pray and anoint the sick person. Anointing with oil – an ancient practice – is not a preparation for death, but on the contrary is here meant to promote health. Elijah, whose prayers were held to have affected the weather, is given as an example of a man of prayer.

*Mark 2.1–12*
Mark describes the healing of a paralysed man in a story which reflects the view generally held at the time that there was a relationship between forgiveness and healing. The story records the opposition aroused when Jesus presumes to be able to forgive sins, the prerogative of God alone. The effectiveness of the healing is taken to be confirmation of the claims of Jesus.

### First year, evening

*II Kings 4.18–37*
This is a story from the life of the prophet Elisha, similar to one told about Elijah, his predecessor. In return for hospitality, Elisha has promised the woman of Shunem a son. Now the son has died, possibly of sunstroke, and Elisha revives him. The story illustrates the Hebrew belief that power can be communicated from one person to another, and shows Elisha to be as powerful a prophet as Elijah

*Mark 3.1–12*
Mark tells a story about Jesus healing on the Sabbath, the recounting of which suggests that the early church was still concerned with the issue of Sabbath observance. This incident and the summary which follows show a belief in Jesus as a great healer, who is able to communicate his power through touch. Together the two parts of the reading illustrate very vividly the contrast between the reaction of the Pharisees and that of the unclean spirits.

## Second year, morning

*II Kings 5.1–14*
This is the story of the healing of Naaman, a successful Syrian general, by the prophet Elisha. It is only when Naaman is willing to follow the prophet's instructions, distasteful though they may be, that he is healed of his leprosy. Elisha the prophet, rather than the king of Israel, is shown to be the means of healing, with the result that Naaman wishes to acknowledge Elisha's God as his own.

*II Corinthians 12.1–10*
In the course of a tempestuous relationship with the church at Corinth, Paul is led to boast about his visions. He recalls one he had fourteen years ago and believes that he was given a physical weakness at about the same time, to prevent the very boasting in which he is now reluctantly engaging. This affliction has led him to trust in God's power rather than his own.

*Mark 1.35–45*
Mark has described Jesus's works of healing, and now puts them in the context of prayer and preaching. He shows how Jesus follows an itinerant ministry. The second half of the passage describes the healing of a leper, in which it is the compassion of Jesus which leads him to heal. The writer includes a mention of Jesus's desire for secrecy, perhaps as an explanation of the fact that Jesus was not universally accepted by the Jews.

## Second year, evening

*Job 2.1–10*
This ancient folk-tale of the affliction of Job describes how he suffers a second calamity: he has already lost goods and family; now he is

smitten with a disfiguring disease. Satan believes that Job's acknowledgment of God is calculated piety, but Job's answer to his wife indicates a deeper understanding of his misfortune: life is of a mixed quality and God is not to be acknowledged as the giver of good things only. Though Satan is later seen as God's adversary, he is here included among the order of semi-divine beings referred to as the sons of God, and his role is to test the sincerity of the righteous.

*Mark 7.24–37*
Mark records two miracle stories. The first concerns the healing of a Gentile girl and shows both the tension in the mind of Jesus about the scope of his ministry and also the way in which he responds to persistent faith. The second – a story found only in Mark's Gospel – contains unusual details of the healing process, and preserves the original Aramaic. A feature of the story is the way in which the command to be silent about the incident leads people to speak of it more.

ASB
**Year 1**

Prefaces as above.

**Year 2**

*II Kings 5.1–14*   Preface as above.

*II Corinthians 12.1–10*   Preface as above.

*Mark 7.24–end*   Preface as above. Second year, evening.

# Seventh Sunday before Easter

*Christ, Worker of Miracles*

## First year, morning

*Deuteronomy 8.1–6*
This passage calls on the Israelites to obey God and to remember the hardships of the forty years in the wilderness, interpreted by the book of Deuteronomy as a discipline to test the obedience of the people. The Israelites are also reminded that it was God who gave them the means of sustenance: manna from heaven, to teach them that man lives not by material things alone, but primarily by God's care.

*Philippians 4.10–20*
Paul thanks the Christians at Philippi for the gift they have sent him, expressing appreciation for their practical help, but even more for their fellowship with him. Somewhat embarrassed by their gift, Paul is anxious that they should not repeat their generosity and emphasizes that their giving was really a sacrifice to God, who is the source of all gifts.

*John 6.1–14*
The writer of John's Gospel tells the story of the feeding of the five thousand which he later uses as the basis for teaching that Jesus is the bread of life. The taking of the loaves, the giving of thanks and the distribution of the bread seem to be a link with the Lord's Supper in the life of the church. The story also shows Jesus to be in charge of what is happening from beginning to end, which is typical of his ministry as recorded in this Gospel.

## First year, evening

*Isaiah 41.8–16*
This passage contains a collection of three separate oracles from the period of the exile. The first is the most important, since it identifies Israel as the servant, a role originally associated with Abraham. This identification may account for the tension in the prophecies between the servant as the nation and as an individual, for Abraham was

both the father of the nation and an individual person. The second oracle restates the familiar prophetic judgment against the nations who are now punishing Israel; the third contrasts the present state of the people with what God is about to do for them.

*John 9.1–25*
The writer of John's Gospel tells the story of the healing of the man who was born blind, a vivid illustration of the claim made in the previous chapter that Jesus is the light of the world. The examination of the healing by the Jews is presented not only as an enquiry into the cure, but more importantly, as an assessment of Jesus. The healed man gives a strong personal testimony.

## Second year, morning

*Jonah 1.1–17*
This passage introduces the story of Jonah, the prophet who is reluctant to obey God's command to preach to the people of Nineveh. The story is told to show that God loves all men, including the Ninevites. It is thus a warning to the Jews living in Jerusalem after the exile not to prevent people of other races from joining them in the worship of God.

*James 1.2–12*
James urges his fellow Christians to regard trials that come to them as a test of their faith. He wants Christians to be perfect, and therefore suggests that his readers should pray in faith to God for wisdom. Steadfastness in the faith is the quality which the writer regards most highly of all.

*Mark 4.35–41*
Mark gives a vivid account of a storm on the lake, in which he contrasts the disciples' fear with the calm of Jesus, who stills the storm. Ability to control the elements is one of the characteristic signs of God's power. This story therefore confronts people with the question of the identity of Jesus and invites a response to him.

## Second year, evening

*Isaiah 30.8–17*
The prophet criticizes the nation for putting its trust in force and deceit, and restates his message of imminent judgment. He believes

that the only hope for the nation is to show its trust in God by ceasing to plot with Egypt. This message is rejected by the people, who do not wish to hear Isaiah talking about God. He is therefore told to write down his prophecies so that God's word, and Isaiah himself, may be vindicated in the future.

*Mark 6.45–56*
This story includes the miracles of walking on the water and stilling the storm, incidents which have a deeper meaning than the literal one. The writer's message is clear: Jesus is both Lord of the sea, sharing with God power over the elements, and the one who comes to his disciples in their time of need.


## ASB
**Year 1**

See Fourth Sunday after Epiphany. First year, morning.

### Year 2

*Numbers 15.32–36*
This is the story of a man who broke the Sabbath law. His action was a deliberate sin, and the law, as stated in the book of Exodus, is clear: he must be put to death by stoning.

*Colossians 1.18–23*
In this hymn in praise of Christ, Paul speaks of Christ's relationship to the created order; he reconciles it to God. Believing Christians are also reconciled to God through the death of Christ.

*John 8.2–11*
This story of the women caught in the act of adultery is probably a later addition to John's Gospel. It illustrates, however, the compassion of Jesus towards sinners and his refusal to give support to the legalism of those who claimed to be righteous.

# Ash Wednesday

## First year, morning

*Isaiah 58.1–8*
The prophet condemns the false religion of the Jerusalem community after the exile, particularly its dependence on fasting unsupported by a righteous life. God is not impressed by mere religious observance. What he requires of his people is the spiritual fast of right conduct, and justice for those who are oppressed, hungry and homeless.

*I Corinthians 9.24–27*
Paul concludes his defence of his ministry with two metaphors, one from racing, the other from boxing. He uses these images, familiar to those visiting the Isthmian games held near Corinth, in his appeal for self-discipline among the Corinthian Christians and as a justification of his own life. They and he together are seeking salvation, a more lasting prize than the olive wreath awarded at the games.

*Matthew 6.16–21*
In this part of the sermon on the mount, the Christian community is first instructed about fasting. Christian fasting is contrasted with the disciplines of the Pharisees in two respects: it is to be joyful – for anointing is a symbol of joy – and it is not to be practised for its effect on men, but is to be directed towards God. Christians are then told that there is much more to life than the hoarding of possessions.

## First year, evening

*Isaiah 1.10–20*
Early in his ministry, perhaps on a feast day, the prophet Isaiah speaks about the worthlessness of mere ritual. This is a familiar and powerful prophetic message : sacrifice, no matter how lavish, is worthless unless accompanied by righteousness. It is not the temple worship, as such, that is being attacked, but rather its separation from everyday conduct. The passage ends with God's offer of forgiveness.

*Mark 2.18–22* See Fifth Sunday after Epiphany. First year, morning.

## Second year, morning

*Amos 5.6–15*
The prophet Amos, speaking at a time of peace and prosperity, attacks corruption in the life of the nation. His message is that God will punish the rich, who have lived at the expense of the poor and needy, and the judges, who have administered false justice 'in the gate', the open-air court at the entrance to the Hebrew village. Amos calls upon the people to return to God, and offers the hope that some – a remnant – will be saved from the destruction which he is sure will come upon the nation.

*James 4.1–8a*
James contrasts the worldly concerns and practices of a Christian community with the lives that should result from living close to God. He argues that it is impossible to be on friendly terms with the world and with God, for God will not accept a divided allegiance. By 'the world' James means not God's creation, which is good, but society in its self-centredness and neglect of God.

*Luke 18.9–14*
In a parable peculiar to Luke's Gospel, the attitude of the Pharisee is contrasted with the response that God requires. The Pharisee is representative of a religious outlook that leads to self-justification and the rejection of others. The tax-collector is representative of that humility, rooted in penitence, which Jesus commends.

## Second year, evening

*Joel 2.12–19*         See Fifth Sunday after Epiphany. First year,
morning.

*II Timothy 2.1–7*
In a series of metaphors, the writer urges Timothy not to give up his discipleship, but to endure and be faithful in his ministry. Perserverance is seen as the characteristic most required in Christian living at a time of suffering and persecution. The passage also gives an indication of the early practice of passing on the message of the gospel from one generation to the next.

*Ash Wednesday*

## ASB
## Years 1 and 2

*Isaiah 58.1–8*   Preface as above.

*Joel 2.12–17*
The prophet Joel reacts to a severe plague of locusts by summoning the people to fasting and repentance and by asking the priests to organize a national day of prayer. The prophet fears not only the disaster the locusts can bring, but also the reaction of the surrounding nations, who will wonder what has happened to Israel's God. But, in response to their repentance, the prophet assures the people of God's forgiveness.

*Amos 5.6 – 15*   Preface as above.

*II Corinthians 9.24–end*   Preface as above.

*James 4.1–10*   Preface as above.

*Matthew 6.16–21*   Preface as above.

*Luke 18.9–14*   Preface as above.

# Sixth Sunday before Easter
(Lent 1)

*The King and the Kingdom: Temptation*

### First year, morning

*Deuteronomy 30.15–20*
In a final message, the writer places before the people the choice
they have to make: obedience to the true God, or idolatry. He urges
them to choose God, confident that such a decision will bring
blessings and long life. But if they decide to worship other gods, all
he can promise them is cursing and death.

*Hebrews 2.14–18*
The writer is seeking to establish the superiority of the high-priesthood of Christ over the priesthood of the Jewish religion, in order
to demonstrate the superiority of Christianity over Judaism. He
therefore asserts that Christ had a real human nature: he suffered
and was tempted. This humanity qualified him to be a sympathetic
high priest.

*Matthew 4.1–17*
Matthew records how the baptism of Jesus is followed by a period of
temptation: it is the Spirit given at baptism who leads Jesus to the
place of testing. The replies that Jesus makes to the temptations are
taken from the book of Deuteronomy, suggesting a parallel between
the forty days Jesus spends in the wilderness and the forty years
spent there by Israel. In all three temptations, the writer shows how
Jesus rejects false interpretations of the sonship which has been
declared at his baptism.

### First year, evening

*Jeremiah 31.27–34*
The prophet Jeremiah assures the exiles in Babylon that God will
rebuild his people and establish a new covenant with them. The old
covenant has been broken by the disobedience and unfaithfulness
of the nation. The new covenant will be spiritual rather than legal,

inward rather than outward, and in it each man will be personally accountable to God.

## Mark 14.1–25

In a highly dramatic series of incidents, Mark weaves different strands into one narrative: the plot to kill Jesus and the betrayal by Judas, the preparation of Jesus for his death by the anointing of his head and the preparation for the feast of the Passover. The passage culminates in the blessing of the bread and wine at the Last Supper, and the interpretation of these actions in terms of a covenant with God.

## Second year, morning

### Deuteronomy 6.10–17

This warning not to forget God follows closely upon the great commandment to love God with heart and soul and might. The passage reflects the knowledge that once they were settled in Canaan, the Israelites did forget this total allegiance demanded by God. The increasing prosperity referred to in this passage caused them to neglect the one true God and worship the gods of the Canaanites.

### Hebrews 4.12–16

The writer of this letter is seeking to establish the superiority of the high priesthood of Christ over the priesthood of the Jewish religion, in order to demonstrate the superiority of Christianity over Judaism. After a reference to the penetrating nature of the word of God, the writer affirms that the exalted Jesus is a high priest who, because of his humanity, is able to understand the human situation. Christians can therefore approach God, through Christ, with confidence.

### Luke 4.1–13

Luke records how the baptism of Jesus is followed by a period of temptation: it is the Spirit given at baptism who leads Jesus to the place of testing. The replies that Jesus makes to the temptations are taken from the book of Deuteronomy, suggesting a parallel between the forty days Jesus spends in the wilderness and the forty years spent there by Israel. In all three temptations, the writer shows how Jesus rejects false interpretations of the sonship which has been declared at his baptism.

## Second year, evening

*Isaiah 58.1–8*   See Ash Wednesday. First year, morning.

*Luke 22.1–38*
Luke writes of a twofold preparation for the Passover: Judas arranges to betray Jesus at a time convenient to the authorities and Peter and John prepare a place for the Passover to be eaten. In this way the scene is set for the Last Supper. Here the theme of betrayal is again prominent, and continues into the final words of Jesus to his disciples, in which he predicts the denial of Peter.


## ASB
## Year 1

*Genesis 2.7–9; 3.1–7*
The first part of this reading is taken from the second of the two creation stories found in the book of Genesis. In Chapter 1 creation is in stages, culminating in the creation of man. Here, God creates man first, by shaping him out of dust and breathing into him the breath of life. The second part of the reading is the story of man's temptation to seek equality with God. The sin of mankind is portrayed through the story of the serpent who deceives the woman and, through her, the man, and, as a result, the Garden of Eden is lost.

*Hebrews 2.14–end*   Preface as above.

*Matthew 4.1–11*   Preface as above.

## Year 2

*Genesis 4.1–10*   See Eighth Sunday before Christmas. Second year, morning.

*Hebrews 4.12–end*   Preface as above.

*Luke 4.1–13*   Preface as above.

# Fifth Sunday before Easter
(Lent 2)

---

*The king and the Kingdom: Conflict*

**First year, morning**

*II Kings 6.8–17*
This story tells how the king of Syria is thwarted in his war against
Israel by Elisha's supernatural knowledge of his military plans. Even
his attempt to capture Elisha is unsuccessful, for the prophet
manages to misdirect the Syrian army to Samaria. The story is told
to testify to Elisha's status as a true prophet, and to illustrate the
belief that God looks after his own people.

*I John 4.1–6*
The writer is seeking to guard the true gospel from distortion, in
particular from that false teaching – here attributed to spirits – which
suggests that Jesus was not truly human. By 'the world' the writer
means not God's creation, which is good, but society in its self
centredness and neglect of God.

*Luke 11.14–26*
Luke writes of the conflict between Jesus and his opponents over
the source of his miraculous power. Jesus, denying that his power is
from an evil source, challenges the people to recognize the working
of God in his ministry and to choose between the kingdom of God
and the powers of evil. 'The finger of God' is a phrase used in Exodus
to describe God's power at work. 'Beelzebul' is the Hebrew name
of a pagan god who became identified in Jewish literature with
Satan. The closing verses about unclean spirits illustrate the truth
that goodness is a positive quality.

**First year, evening**

*Isaiah 59.1–16*
In a lament expressing the community's distress, the prophet de
scribes the situation in Jerusalem after the exile. There has been
bloodshed; lying and injustice have been practised in the law courts;
the innocent have suffered and the honest have been powerless to

ntervene. The prophet therefore makes confession to God, and nticipates that he will reassert his justice and punish the wicked.

*Mark 14.26–52*

The passion narrative in the Gospel of Mark includes the theme of betrayal: the desertion of the disciples is forecast, their inability to stay awake while Jesus prays is described, the moment of betrayal by Judas is vividly portrayed and the passage concludes with a brief reference to a young man who also ran away. As the time of testing comes to a head, all are shown to have deserted Jesus, and he is led away to his trial and death alone.

## Second year, morning

*Isaiah 35.1–10*

The prophet describes the day of salvation: it will include the transformation of nature and the building of a new highway along which God will lead his people home to Jerusalem. There is a great contrast between this picture and the description of God's judgment given in the previous chapter: there his judgment burned up the countryside, here the desert itself will blossom. This is a message of hope to those in exile: God will rescue his people.

*John 3.1–8*

In a passage which illustrates conflict in the community between the children of God and their opponents, the writer seeks to make clear what it means to be a child of God. It means being like Christ and this demands purity. The writer rejects the false teaching that sin is of little account. On the contrary, sin is literally devilish. The situation out of which the author writes leaves him no room for compromise or concession to human weakness.

*Matthew 12.22–32*

Matthew describes how the healing power of Jesus is attributed by the Pharisees to the power of evil. Jesus declares that, on the contrary, he casts out evil by the Spirit of God. In calling good, evil, the Pharisees are committing the unforgivable sin. Furthermore, the reference to the sin against the Holy Spirit suggests that, while it is to be expected that some will not recognize Jesus as Messiah during his ministry, after Pentecost, when the Holy Spirit has been given, there will be no excuse.

*Fifth Sunday before Easter*

## Second year, evening

### Genesis 37.12–28
This is the story of the sale of Joseph by his brothers into slavery in Egypt. The incident is the outcome of the jealousy of the brothers, caused by the favouritism shown to Joseph by their father, Israel. The long robe with sleeves was the symbol of this favouritism. The story is part of the saga of how the Israelites went down into Egypt, from which God later rescued them in the exodus.

### Luke 22.39–53
Luke continues his account of the passion of Christ with two related events, both taking place in the garden of Gethsemane. The first is the agonizing of Jesus and the strength he receives in prayer. The second is the betrayal by Judas and the arrest of Jesus. Both events illustrate the struggle between the powers of evil and the will of God, and are recorded by Luke to strengthen the church in times of temptation and struggle.

## ASB
## Year 1

*Genesis 6.11 – end*    See Fifth Sunday before Christmas. First year, evening.

*I John 4.1–6*    Preface as above.

*Luke 19.41 – end*
In the course of his entry into Jerusalem, Jesus weeps over the city. He knows that the people's coming rejection of him will lead to their disaster. The passage ends with the cleansing of the temple and the rulers' search for ways to destroy him.

## Year 2

*Genesis 7.17 – end*
The story of the flood describes the destruction of all creatures except those on the ark with Noah. The writer uses this story to indicate the consequences of the rejection of God's rule: the break-up of the created order.

74

*I John 3.1–8*   Preface as above.

*Matthew 12.22–32*   Preface as above.

# Fourth Sunday before Easter
(Lent 3)

## The King and the Kingdom: Suffering

### First year, morning

*Isaiah 59.15–20*
The prophet has described the conditions of injustice in the country after the return from exile. Now, speaking of God as a warrior, he expresses his belief that God himself will intervene and fight for righteousness. This action will result not only in God being known to his people as their Redeemer, but also in his recognition throughout the world.

*I Peter 2.19–25*
In a message addressed to Christian slaves, the writer urges willing acceptance of humiliation and suffering. In this way slaves will be following the example of Christ, who suffered for them. There are echoes here of the suffering servant of Isaiah chapter 53, a prophecy which influenced the understanding of Christ's suffering and death in some early Christian communities.

*Matthew 16.13–28*
Matthew records Peter's confession that Jesus is Messiah and the rebuke he receives from Jesus. The incident illustrates Peter's importance in the early church and indicates the authority he exercised. Then follows a call to Christian discipleship and to an acceptance of suffering within the Christian community. The passage concludes with a reference to the return of Christ in glory, a feature of early Christian belief.

### First year, evening

*Jeremiah 2.1–13*
The prophet Jeremiah reminds the people of their history and claims that, although at first they responded to God's care with devotion, they have now ungratefully forgotten what he has done for them. In the vivid image of the water cistern, Jeremiah condemns their rejection of God and the way they have turned to other gods.

*Mark 14.53–72*
Mark records the trial of Jesus by the Jews and Peter's denial, a denial which stands in marked contrast to the confession Jesus makes himself. The account of the trial emphasizes the absence of defence witnesses and the silence of Jesus. It is only when Jesus responds with what seems to be a clear acceptance of his role as Messiah that the Jews are able to condemn him.

## Second year, morning

*Isaiah 45.18–25*
In this chapter, the prophet contrasts the God of Israel with the idols worshipped by other nations. He acknowledges that God is often hidden, but affirms the reality of his presence in his spoken word and in his creation. God is a righteous God, offering salvation to the whole world.

*Colossians 1.24–29*
Paul speaks of his share in Christ's sufferings. He may be referring to his own pain as a share in Christ's suffering, or he may be thinking of suffering to be endured within the church before the day of the Lord comes. He then speaks of his ministry of preaching Christ to the Gentiles. It is to this universal mission, God's open secret made known in Christ, that he has given his life.

*Luke 9.18–27*
Luke relates Peter's confession of Jesus as God's anointed one, and uses it as an opportunity to record Jesus's teaching about his coming death. Then follows a call to Christian discipleship and to an acceptance of suffering within the Christian community. The passage concludes with a reference to the return of Christ in glory, a feature of early Christian belief.

## Second year, evening

*Micah 7.1–7*
Micah prophesied at the close of the eighth century BC, when great political events were taking place, but unlike his contemporary Isaiah, he shows little interest in them. Instead, he condemns the injustice of the rulers of Jerusalem and the mistrust to be found in

*Fourth Sunday before Easter*

families; he can see no godly person left. Despite such pessimism, the prophet himself will continue to trust in God.

*Luke 22.54–71*
Luke records Peter's denial of Jesus and the examination of Jesus by the Jewish leaders. The story makes it clear that the real point at issue in the trial is the messiahship of Jesus. Jesus does not deny the titles Messiah or Son of God, but accepts them by implication.

## ASB
### Year 1

*Genesis 22.1–13*   See Seventh Sunday before Christmas. Second year, morning.

*Colossians 1.24 – end*   Preface as above.

*Luke 9.18–27*   Preface as above.

### Year 2

*Genesis 12.1–9*   See Seventh Sunday before Christmas. First year, morning.

*I Peter 2.19 – end*   Preface as above.

*Matthew 16.13 – end*   Preface as above.

# Third Sunday before Easter
(Lent 4)

*The King and the Kingdom: Transfiguration*

## First year, morning

*Exodus 34.29–35*
This is the story of Moses coming down from the mountain, his face shining with the reflection of divine glory. The story is told by the priests in Jerusalem after the exile and they often speak of the presence of God in terms of brightness and light.

*II Corinthians 3.12–18*
Paul's interpretation of the veil that Moses put over his face is different from that given in the book of Exodus. Paul says that by means of the veil, Moses was hiding from the people the fact that the glory reflected in his face was fading. In this interpretation, Paul is trying to show that the knowledge of God in Judaism is veiled. Unlike Moses, Christians can openly reflect the glory of God, because they are being transformed by the Spirit of the Lord.

*Matthew 17.1–13*
In the story of the transfiguration, three disciples are given a special revelation of the glory of God in Christ. The story seems related to the Jewish feast of Tabernacles or Booths – a booth was a hut in the vineyard or orchard at harvest time. The transfiguration is used to signify the coming of the new age when Jesus will be enthroned in glory. The conversation of Jesus with the disciples on their way down from the mountain confirms that he is to be understood in terms of both suffering and victory. There is also a reference to the Jewish tradition that Elijah would appear just before the Messiah came.

## First year, evening

*Isaiah 52.13–53.6*
The prophet speaks of his vision of the righteous servant of God who shares the sufferings of the people and bears their sin. The theme of such suffering for others is presented here in intensely

personal terms, and yet the servant is also to be understood as representing the true Israel. The passage offers the people not only forgiveness for their sin but also a mission of suffering on behalf of others.

*Mark 15.1–20*
Mark's account of the trial of Jesus before Pilate emphasizes the reluctance with which Pilate orders the crucifixion. He acts against his better judgment, and indeed wishes to release Jesus rather than Barabbas. The attitude of Pilate towards Jesus was important to the early church, which sought to show that, from the beginning, the Roman authorities had no real quarrel with Christianity. The silence of Jesus at his trial is an example for Christians who were themselves put on trial.

## Second year, morning

*I Kings 19.1–12*
After his victory over the prophets of Baal on Mount Carmel, Elijah flees from Jezebel's threats to kill him. He is full of self-pity, thinking that he alone is faithful to God. He expects God to show his support by appearing to him on Mount Horeb in some dramatic way. But God speaks to him in a soft whisper.

*II Peter 1.16–19*
The writer claims to have been an eyewitness of the transfiguration of Christ. This means he can assure his readers that he is speaking the truth when he tells them of the present power of Christ and of his future coming. One of the themes of the letter is that the transfiguration confirms Jewish prophecies about the coming of Christ.

*Luke 9.28–36*
Luke has already claimed that Christ's glory will be seen through his sufferings and death. This glory is now confirmed by the transfiguration, in which Moses and Elijah appear as the representatives of the Jewish law and prophets. It is in accord with the interests of this Gospel that prayer should be the setting of this story.

**Second year, evening**

*Jeremiah 30.12–17*
Jeremiah reminds the people that their suffering is deserved: it is
God's judgment on them for their wickedness. But this message to
the exiles contains a note of hope, too, for the prophet believes that
God will defeat Israel's enemies and restore her to health. The
passage therefore reflects both the judgment and the mercy of God.

*Luke 23.1–25*
Luke's account of the passion of Jesus now turns to his trial by Pilate,
into which is inserted the appearance before Herod. Luke details
the charge brought against Jesus and underlines both his innocence
of any political crimes and Pilate's desire to release him.

# ASB
## Year 1

*Exodus 34.29 – end*   Preface as above.

*II Corinthians 3.4 – end*
After referring to the confident faith of the Christian, Paul contrasts
the splendour of the old dispensation with that of the new. His
interpretation of the veil that Moses put over his face is different
from that given in the book of Exodus. Paul says that by means of
the veil, Moses was hiding from the people the fact that the glory
reflected in his face was fading. In this interpretation, Paul is trying
to show that the knowledge of God in Judaism is veiled. Unlike
Moses, Christians can openly reflect the glory of God, because they
are being transformed by the Spirit of the Lord.

*Luke 9.28–36*   Preface as above.

## Year 2

*Exodus 3.1–6*
The story of the burning bush describes in symbolic terms Moses'
encounter with God. Later in the account of this experience, Moses
is called to secure the freedom of his people and God discloses to
him the name that signifies his own mysterious nature.

*II Peter 1.16–19*   Preface as above.

# Second Sunday before Easter
(Passion Sunday)

## The King and the Kingdom: Victory of the Cross

### First year, morning

*Isaiah 63.1–9*
The prophet announces the day of God's vengeance on the enemies of Israel. God is depicted as coming from Edom, a special enemy of Israel who constantly attacked her. The picture therefore is of God as a blood-stained warrior coming to destroy the enemy and to bring salvation to his people.

*Colossians 2.8–15*
Paul describes what the death of Christ has achieved. Through baptism, Christians share in both the death and resurrection of Christ and are no longer tied to the Jewish law with its demand of circumcision. In a dramatic image, Paul says that, when Jesus was nailed to the cross, he destroyed the indictment which convicted man of sin. He sees the crucifixion as the decisive battle against the powers of evil, in which they were disarmed and defeated.

*John 12.20–32*
The writer of John's Gospel uses the incident of Greeks seeking Jesus to show that the world-wide mission of the Christian faith is dependent upon the death of Christ. His death is therefore described as his moment of glory, and the cross as the means by which he will draw all men to himself.

### First year, evening

*Isaiah 53.7–12*
The prophet has described the servant as the bearer of the sin of the people. Now, perhaps drawing on his own experience, he describes the suffering of the servant culminating in his death. This he interprets as an offering for sin, and declares it to be an expression of the will of God. Through the action of the servant, God's intention for his people will be fulfilled and Israel will be saved.

*Mark 15.21–41*
Mark describes the crucifixion of Jesus. The story details the last incidents in the life of Jesus and contrasts his rejection by the Jewish leaders with the confession of faith made by the centurion. This confession echoes the opening claim of the Gospel, that Jesus is the Son of God.

## Second year, morning

*Jeremiah 31.31–34*
The prophet Jeremiah assures the exiles in Babylon that God will establish a new covenant with them. The old covenant has been broken by the disobedience and unfaithfulness of the nation. The new covenant will be spiritual rather than legal, inward rather than outward, and in it each man will be personally accountable to God.

*Hebrews 9.11–15*
The writer, using the language of Jewish sacrifice, contrasts the priesthood of Jesus with the Jewish priesthood. He does this in order to assert the superiority of Christianity over Judaism. Here, the particular point of contrast is the sacrifice offered: the Jewish high priest could sacrifice only the blood of animals, and that annually; Jesus, both priest and victim, has sacrificed his own blood once for all. This is a pure sacrifice, a perfect redemption, and therefore effective for establishing a new relationship with God.

*Mark 10.32–45*
Mark introduces the final stage of the journey to Jerusalem with a detailed prediction of what is to happen to Jesus there. The disciples' failure to understand is well illustrated in the attempt by James and John to claim for themselves places of honour. The quarrel between the disciples gives rise to sayings about the nature of Christian living and about the death of Jesus himself. Mark understands Jesus's death as a 'ransom', a word probably meaning 'deliverance' rather than 'payment'.

## Second year, evening

*Lamentations 1.1–14*
The book of Lamentations reflects the situation of those left in Judah after the Babylonian forces had destroyed Jerusalem and

taken its leading citizens into exile. In the opening poem, the leader of this broken community laments over these disasters, and interprets them as divine judgment on the sins of the people. He condemns political alliances, lifeless worship and rebellion against God's rule, and exclaims that God has hung these sins around Judah's neck to convict her of her sin.

*Luke 23.26–49*
Luke describes the scene of the crucifixion. He introduces into it the lament over Jerusalem: the city will suffer disaster as a result of its rejection of Jesus. The wailing women should therefore keep their pity for themselves. Luke has also brought into the story the comments of the two men crucified at the same time as Jesus, and he uses the incident to illustrate his persistent theme that the outcasts, represented here by a criminal, will enter the kingdom first.


## ASB
**Year 1**

*Exodus 6.2–13*   See Sixth Sunday before Christmas. Second year morning.

*Colossians 2.8–15*   Preface as above.

*John 12.20–32*   Preface as above.

**Year 2**

Prefaces as above.

# The Sunday before Easter
(Palm Sunday)

*The Way of the Cross*

## First year, morning

*Zechariah 9.9–12*
The prophet shares his vision that in a new age to come, Jerusalem will be ruled by a king who is both triumphant and humble. The prophecy comes from a time when the Jews were experiencing much distress and uncertainty, and expresses the belief that God will bring in an age of prosperity and peace. The 'River' referred to is the River Euphrates.

*I Corinthians 1.18–25*
Paul seeks to raise the Corinthians above party strife by reminding them of his central belief in the power of the cross. Jewish and Greek opponents are told of the irrelevance of signs to convince them and wisdom to persuade them. Christ who was crucified is the expression of the wisdom and power of God.

*Mark 11.1–11*
Mark describes the entry of Jesus into Jerusalem as a fulfilment of the prophecy of Zechariah, and therefore as a claim to be Messiah. The action of Jesus once he was in the city, described in the final verse of the passage, must have appeared as an anticlimax to the crowd. But it is an indication that Jesus was not willing to fulfil the popular understanding of what it meant to be Messiah.

*Mark 15.21–39* See Second Sunday before Easter. First year, evening.

## First year, evening

*Isaiah 56.1–8*
This passage reflects the problems of the Jewish community after the return from exile. The prophet urges the people to worship in the temple and to observe the Sabbath, for this is obedience to the law of God. Eunuchs had no place in worship, as they could not

father children and so add to the community, and foreigners were excluded from the temple. But here the prophet states that the temple is to be for all people.

*Mark 11.12–33*
Mark describes the cleansing of the temple and the cursing and withering of the fig-tree. The cleansing of the temple is a sign that the kingdom of God has come. The cursing of the fig-tree is a parable of Jesus's rejection of the barrenness of Jewish religion. Both incidents raise the question of the authority of Jesus, which is treated explicitly in the concluding verses. The method of responding to one question by asking another was common among the rabbis.

## Second year, morning

*Isaiah 52.13–53.12*   See Third Sunday before Easter. First year, evening.

*Hebrews 10.1–10*
In this passage, the Jewish religion, with its stress on law and sacrifice, is said to be but a shadow of what is revealed in Christ. He has overcome the inadequacy of the Jewish sacrificial system through his obedience to the will of God and his perfect sacrifice. The quotation is from Psalm 40.

*Matthew 21.1–11*
Matthew describes the entry of Jesus into Jerusalem as a fulfilment of the prophecy of Zechariah, and therefore as a claim to be Messiah. In this Gospel, the entry provokes reaction in the whole city, and there is an immediate demand to know the identity of Jesus.

*Matthew 27.32–54*
Matthew tells the story of the crucifixion of Jesus as king of the Jews. The story is partly about Jesus, his loneliness and his cry of despair, but it is also about reactions to him. The passers-by taunt him; the Jewish leaders mock him; the thieves revile him. According to Matthew, creation responds to his death in a supernatural way, anticipating what the Jews believed would happen at the end of the world. The centurion and those with him make the confession of faith: Jesus is the Son of God.

**Second year, evening**

*Isaiah 5.1–7*

In a striking poem, Isaiah tells the parable of the vineyard, a popular ballad which may well have been sung at a festival. Its real meaning is concealed until the end: Israel, the vineyard, is condemned because she has yielded no fruit. God has cared for his people, but their only response has been injustice and oppression. What is he to do but leave them to their fate?

*Mark 12.1–12*

Mark takes up from Jewish scripture the metaphor of the vineyard. He compares the Jewish people to the tenants who refused to let the owner have his fruit and rejected his messengers. The son who was finally sent is clearly meant to be Jesus, and this is why the Jewish leaders, who hear the story, wish to arrest him.

# ASB
## Years 1 and 2

*Isaiah 50.4–9a*   See Thirteenth Sunday after Pentecost. First year, morning.

*Philippians 2.5–11*   See Christmas Day. Second year, evening.

*Mark 14.32–15.41*

Mark records the agony of Jesus in Gethsemane, his arrest and trial, the denial of Peter, the release of Barabbas and the crucifixion itself. In the account there is a contrast between the rejection of Jesus by the Jewish authorities and the confession of faith made by the centurion. This confession echoes the opening claim of the Gospel, that Jesus is the Son of God.

*Zechariah 9.9–12*   Preface as above.

*1 Corinthians 1.18–25*   Preface as above.

*Matthew 21.1–13*

Matthew describes the entry of Jesus into Jerusalem as a fulfilment of the prophecy of Zechariah, and therefore as a claim to be Messiah. In this gospel, the entry provokes reaction in the whole city, and there is an immediate demand to know the identity of Jesus. Jesus then cleanses the temple, an act which demonstrates his identity as Messiah.

# Monday in Holy Week

## Years 1 and 2

*Isaiah 42.1–7* See First Sunday after Epiphany. Second year, morning.

*Hebrews 2.9–18*
The writer of this letter, quoting from the Old Testament, is arguing that Jesus is superior to the angels. He is also seeking to establish the superiority of the high priesthood of Christ to the priesthood of the Jewish religion, in order to demonstrate the superiority of Christianity to Judaism. He therefore asserts that Christ had a real human nature: he suffered and was tempted. This humanity qualified him to be a sympathetic high priest.

*Matthew 26.1–30*
This is the account of the preparation for the feast of the Passover and of the way in which Jesus celebrated it with his disciples. It contains within it the plans to kill Jesus and his betrayal by Judas to the authorities. The story of the anointing of Jesus is a symbol of what is to come: it is a preparation for his burial.

*Luke 22.1–38* See Sixth Sunday before Easter. Second year, evening.

# Tuesday in Holy Week

## Years 1 and 2

*Isaiah 49.1–6*   See Epiphany. First year.

*Hebrews 8.1–6*   See Sixth Sunday before Christmas. Second year, evening. Preface for Hebrews 8.1–12.

*Matthew 26.31 – end*
Matthew begins this passage with the prophecy of Peter's denial and ends it with the denial itself. Between the two he records the agony of Jesus in Gethsemane, his arrest and his trial.

*Luke 22.39 – end*
Luke continues his account of the passion of Christ with two related events, both taking place in the garden of Gethsemane. The first is the agonizing of Jesus and the strength he receives in prayer. The second is the betrayal by Judas and the arrest of Jesus. Both events illustrate the struggle between the powers of evil and the will of God, and are recorded by Luke to strengthen the church in times of temptation and struggle. Then follow the denial of Peter, the mocking and beating of Jesus and his appearance before the Sanhedrin.

# Wednesday in Holy Week

## Years 1 and 2

*Isaiah 50.4–9a*   See Thirteenth Sunday after Pentecost. First year, morning.

*I Peter 2.19 – end*   See Fourth Sunday before Easter. First year, morning.

*Matthew 27.1–56*
This passage records the suicide of Judas, the trial of Jesus before Pilate, the release of Barabbas and the passion and death of Jesus. Matthew writes of the reactions of the witnesses and introduces miraculous elements into his account of what follows the crucifixion.

*Luke 23.1–49*
Luke's account of the passion of Jesus now turns to his trial by Pilate, into which is inserted the appearance before Herod. Luke details the charge brought against Jesus and underlines both his innocence of any political crimes and Pilate's desire to release him. He then describes the scene of the crucifixion, introducing into it the lament over Jerusalem: the city will suffer disaster as a result of its rejection of Jesus. The wailing women should therefore keep their pity for themselves. Luke has also brought into the story the comments of the two men crucified at the same time as Jesus, and he uses the incident to illustrate his persistent theme that the outcasts, represented here by a criminal, will enter the kingdom first.

# Thursday before Easter
(Maundy Thursday)

## The Upper Room

### First year

*Isaiah 52.13–53.12*   See Third Sunday before Easter. First year, evening.

*I Corinthians 11.23–29*
This passage is the earliest written account of the Last Supper. Paul reminds the Christians at Corinth of the tradition he has already passed on to them concerning its celebration. There is a strong note of judgment in Paul's understanding of the Last Supper: self-examination is necessary before the feast.

*John 13.1–15*
The writer of John's Gospel tells of Jesus washing the feet of his disciples during the course of his last meal with them on the eve of the Passover. Peter's objection to Jesus doing this menial task for him is typical of the disciples' failure to understand the character of Jesus: he is their Lord and therefore serves them; he is their teacher and therefore gives them an example. To the writer, the washing of the feet is a parable of the cleansing offered by Christ through his death.

### Second year

*Jeremiah 31.31–34*
The prophet Jeremiah assures the exiles in Babylon that God will rebuild his people and establish a new covenant with them. The old covenant has been broken by the disobedience and unfaithfulness of the nation. The new covenant will be spiritual rather than legal, and inward rather than outward.

*I Corinthians 10.16–17*
Paul explains to the Corinthians that sharing in the Lord's Supper is more than eating a meal together. It involves unity with Christ and with one another.

*Mark 14.12–26*
Jesus tells his disciples at the Last Supper that one of them will betray him. He blesses the bread and wine and gives an interpretation of these actions in terms of a covenant with God.

## ASB
## Years 1 and 2

*Exodus 12.1–14* See Good Friday. First and Second years, morning.

*I Corinthians 11.23–29* Preface as above.

*John 13.1–15* Preface as above.

## ASB
## The Blessing of the Oils

*Isaiah 61.1–9* See Sunday after Christmas. Second year, evening.

*James 5.13–16a* See Eighth Sunday before Easter. First year, morning.

*Revelation 1.5b–8*
The author opens his letters to the seven churches with this acknowledgement of the glory of Jesus and the eternal nature of God.

*Luke 4.16–21* See Third Sunday before Christmas. Second year, morning.

# Good Friday

## The Death of Christ

### First and Second years, morning

*Exodus 12.1–8,11*
The writer describes the feast of the Passover. This feast, celebrated in the spring, probably began as a sacrifice of the first-born animals, but was later interpreted, as in this passage, as a commemoration of the deliverance of the Israelites from Egypt. In the memory of the people, the exodus was universally honoured and the feast of the Passover became a family festival.

*Hebrews 10.11–25*
The writer contrasts the priestly work of Christ with that of the Jewish priest. The latter's work is never done, but Christ's sacrifice is now complete and, as Messiah, he is glorified with God. The true worship of God, therefore, is to be offered through Christ.

*John 19.17–30*
In this account of the crucifixion of Jesus, the writer of John's Gospel emphasizes the kingship of Christ, a kingship proclaimed to the whole world by the notice, in three languages, on the cross. There are three words spoken from the cross: in the first, Jesus commits his mother to the care of John, perhaps thought of as a representative of the believing community; the second word illustrates the reality of what is happening to the human Jesus: he thirsts; in the third, 'It is finished', Jesus triumphantly affirms that his work is now complete.

### First year, evening

*Job 19.21–20.5*
Job's unhappy position has created a sense of loneliness: even his closest friends have turned against him. He is desperate. But in two verses, in which some of the original Hebrew words are not known, he makes the affirmation that after his death he will see God.

*John 19.31–42*
The writer of John's Gospel explains that, because Jesus is already dead, it is unnecessary to break his legs, though his side is pierced by

a spear. This is seen as the fulfilment of a Jewish prophecy. The water and the blood symbolize, for the writer, the sacraments of baptism and the Lord's Supper. In Christian belief, both are dependent on the death of Jesus.

## Second year, evening

*Lamentations 3.1–9, 19–33*
Jerusalem has been destroyed and its rulers deported. The leader of the Jewish community left behind, laments on behalf of his people : God has punished them and there is no hope for them. But out of this deep despair arises new hope, based on a knowledge of God's mercy and faithful love. Two possible reactions to calamity and suffering are therefore to be found in this passage: a hopeless bitterness and rejection of God, and a hopeful remembrance of his grace.

*Luke 23.50–56*
Luke tells of the burial of Jesus by Joseph of Arimathea. Joseph, a leading Jew, represents those Jews who responded to Jesus. The scene is also set for the resurrection: the women carefully note the tomb where Jesus is laid and go home to prepare for anointing his body.

## ASB
## Years 1 and 2

*Isaiah 52.13–53 end*
The prophet speaks of his vision of the righteous servant of God who shares the sufferings of the people and bears their sin. The theme of such suffering for others is presented here in intensely personal terms, and yet the servant is also to be understood as representing the true Israel. The passage offers the people not only forgiveness for their sin but also a mission of suffering on behalf of others. The suffering of the servant culminates in his death, interpreted by the writer as an offering for sin.

*Hebrews 10.1–25 or 10.12–22*    Preface as above for Hebrews 10.11–25.

## Good Friday

*Hebrews 4.14–16; 5.7–9*
The writer of this letter is seeking to establish the superiority of the high priesthood of Christ over the priesthood of the Jewish religion, in order to demonstrate the superiority of Christianity over Judaism. He affirms that the exalted Jesus is a high priest who, because of his humanity, is able to understand the human situation. Christians can therefore approach God, through Christ, with confidence.

*John 18.1–19, 37*
This is John's account of the arrest and trial of Jesus. The story not only recounts what happened to Jesus but also shows how he was in fact in control of events.

*John 19.1–37*
This is John's account of the crucifixion. It follows the trial before Pilate and shows how Pilate wishes to release Jesus but is prevented by the Jews. The theme of the fulfilment of Jewish scripture plays an important part in the way the story is told.

# Easter Eve

## Years 1 and 2

*Job 14.1–14*
This passage is part of Job's reply to his friends. It reflects man's tragic position, his temporary existence and his ultimate extinction. Yet within this hopelessness there is expressed a longing that existence in the underworld after death might in some way be life with God. Job's waiting now has an element of hope.

*1 Peter 3.17 – end*
The author looks back to the passion of Christ as an example to those now suffering and interprets his death and resurrection by reference to the practice of baptism. He refers explicitly to the interval between Christ's death and resurrection as a time when Christ preached to sinners who had formerly died, including those drowned in the flood, an event seen as a foreshadowing of Christian baptism.

*Matthew 27.57 – end*
Following his death, Jesus is buried in a tomb nearby. This passage records the burial, those who witnessed it, and the precautions taken by the Jewish leaders to secure the tomb.

*John 2.18–22*
When his authority is challenged, Jesus causes consternation by speaking of the destruction and rebuilding of the temple, interpreted here as the destruction of his own body, the place where God's Spirit dwells. The writer stresses that it will only be after the resurrection that the meaning of Jesus's words will become clear to the disciples.

# Easter Day

*The Resurrection of Christ*

### First year, morning

*Isaiah 12.1–6*
The prophet Isaiah joyfully proclaims the greatness of God in a song which tells how God will comfort and deliver his people. It is a song of thanksgiving, inviting the people of Jerusalem to make known throughout the world the mighty works of God.

*Revelation 1.12–18*
A Christian prophet here describes, in strange symbolic language, his vision of the risen Christ. While he was in a trance, a voice had told him to write to the seven churches, and on turning to see who spoke, the prophet saw the vision he describes. The prophet's message is: Christ is alive and will be alive for evermore; in him is to be found the key to life and death.

*Mark 16.1–8*
Mark tells how the women come to the tomb, where the body of Jesus has been placed, and find it empty. But the story is not just of an empty tomb; it is a story of faith, for the young man, or angel, who speaks to the women, affirms the resurrection of Jesus. The women respond with astonishment to what they see and hear, but keep silent because they are afraid.

### First and Second years, morning (alternatives)

*Exodus 14.15–22*
The people of Israel have escaped from Egypt, but the Egyptian army pursues them. This passage tells the story of the parting of the waters and the crossing of the Red Sea. The exodus is the greatest event in Hebrew tradition and is continually recalled in Jewish scripture. God has acted to save his people, and such a God can be trusted to act again.

*I Corinthians 15.12–20*
Paul has recited the evidence for the resurrection, listing the appearances of the risen Christ. Now he calls on the Corinthians to

believe both in the resurrection of Christ and in their own. In speaking of Christ as the first fruits, Paul refers to the Jewish custom of presenting the first fruits of the harvest in the temple, and uses the image to present the risen Christ as the forerunner of all Christian believers.

*John 20.1–18*
The writer of John's Gospel tells the story of the discovery of the empty tomb and of the first appearance of the risen Jesus.

## First year, evening

*Isaiah 26.1–9*
This passage is a song celebrating victory over Israel's enemies and the deliverance of Jerusalem. It praises God who has defended Israel and brought his people home victorious. The prophet sees the possibility of a great future for Israel, if the people rely upon God.

*Luke 24.1–12*
Luke tells the story of the empty tomb. It is discovered by the same women who followed Jesus in Galilee; they are witnesses both to his ministry and to his resurrection. But the women's account of what they have seen is not believed; it is only when the disciples experience the resurrection for themselves that they respond in faith.

## Second year, morning

*Isaiah 12.1–6*   See Easter Day. First year, morning.

*I Corinthians 5.7b–8*
In a passage rebuking the Corinthian Christians for tolerating immorality within the life of the church, Paul urges them to throw out the old leaven and be renewed by Christ: Christ crucified and risen. The unleavened bread suggests newness and purity: these are the marks of the resurrection community.

*Matthew 28.1–10*
Matthew tells, in his own way, the story of the discovery of the empty tomb, including an earthquake. The angel's proclamation of the resurrection is confirmed for the women by the appearance of

*Easter Day*

Jesus. Their reaction is to worship him: this was the response of faith within the Christian community which recognized the risen Jesus as Lord.

## Second year, evening

*Isaiah 42.10–16*
The prophet bursts forth in praise because there is a new king over Israel. His hope is that God will be at work in the reign of this king and will renew the life of Israel. In response to this song, God himself speaks, using the image of childbirth to express his activity. He will come in judgment and in blessing to his people.

*Luke 24.13–35*
Luke tells the story of how the risen Jesus appears to two disciples on the road to Emmaus, and how he makes himself known to them. The story affirms that the Jewish scriptures have already spoken about Christ and that an understanding of his sufferings and death can be found there. The meal that Jesus shares with the two disciples resembles the Last Supper, and the story proclaims that in the breaking of the bread Christians can experience the presence of the risen Lord.

## ASB
## Years 1 and 2

*Isaiah 12*   Preface as above.

*Exodus 14.15–22*   Preface as above.

*Isaiah 43.16–21*
The prophet proclaims that the God who brought the Isarelites out of Egypt will rescue his people again.

*Revelation 1.10–18*   Preface as above.

*I Corinthians 15.12.20*   Preface as above.

*Colossians 3.1–11*   See Third Sunday after Easter. Second year, morning.

*Matthew 28.1–10*   Preface as above.

*John 20.1–10*
The writer of John's Gospel tells the story of the discovery of the empty tomb.

*John 20.1–18*   Preface as above.

*Mark 16.1–8*   Preface as above.

ASB

# Monday in Easter Week

## Years 1 and 2

*Isaiah 42.10–16*   See Easter Day. Second year, evening.

*I Peter 1.1–12*   See Sunday after Easter. First year, morning.
Preface for I Peter 1.3–9.

*Luke 24.13–35*   See Easter Day. Second year, evening.

# Tuesday in Easter Week

## Years 1 and 2

*Micah 7.7 – end*   See Twentieth Sunday after Pentecost. Second year, evening. Preface for Micah 7.7–10a; 18–20.

*I Peter 1.13 – end*   See Fourth Sunday after Easter. First year, evening. Preface for I Peter 1.10–21.

*Luke 24.36–49*
Luke closes his Gospel with the charge given by the risen Christ to his disciples, that they should witness to his fulfilment of the Jewish scriptures. They are to preach repentance and forgiveness throughout the world, thus continuing the ministry of Jesus himself. The Gospel ends, as it began, with the people waiting for the kingdom of God.

# Wednesday in Easter Week

## Years 1 and 2

*1 Kings 17.17 – end*   See Third Sunday after Easter. Second year morning.

*1 Peter 2.1–10*   See Second Sunday after Pentecost. First year morning.

*John 20.24 – end*
The writer of John's Gospel records an appearance of the risen Jesus to his disciples, and the sceptical Thomas makes his confession of faith: Jesus is Lord. The writer records that Jesus showed his wounds to the disciples, for he wishes to make clear that it really is the man Jesus, and not a phantom.

ASB

# Thursday in Easter Week

## Years 1 and 2

*Jeremiah 31.1–14* See Fourth Sunday before Christmas. Second year, evening. Preface for Jeremiah 31.7–14.

*1 Peter 2.11 – end*
The writer makes a plea for good conduct and for responsible behaviour as citizens. He then addresses Christian slaves, recommending to them the willing acceptance of humiliation and suffering. In this way slaves will be following the example of Christ, who suffered for them. There are echoes here of the suffering servant of Isaiah chapter 53, a prophecy which influenced the understanding of Christ's suffering and death in some early Christian communities.

*John 21.1–14* See Second Sunday after Easter. Second year, evening.

ASB

# Friday in Easter Week

## Years 1 and 2

*Ezekiel 37.1–14* See Eighth Sunday after Pentecost. Second year, evening.

*I Peter 3.1–12* See Fifteenth Sunday after Pentecost. Second year, morning. Preface for I Peter 3.1–9.

*John 21.15–17*
In this passage the risen Jesus reinstates Peter with a threefold question and commission.

ASB

# Saturday in Easter Week

*Job 14.1–14*   See Easter Eve. Preface for ASB.

*I Peter 4.1–11*
This passage speaks of the suffering of Christians in making their witness to the world. The writer also urges his readers to show love to one another in view of the early Christian belief in the nearness of the end of the world, with its inevitable judgment.

*John 21.20 – end*
Peter asks the risen Jesus about the beloved disciple, whose identity is not known, but whose role is to witness to the truth of this Gospel.

# The Sunday after Easter

## *The Upper Room Appearances*

### First year, morning

*Exodus 15.1–11*
In a triumphal song, Moses and the people celebrate God's victory over the Egyptians. The song, which was later used in worship in the temple, celebrates the chief incident in the exodus, the most important event in history of Israel. God is depicted as a mighty warrior who is able to overcome the enemy and control the forces of nature.

*I Peter 1.3–9*
In a letter addressed to Christians in the Roman world, the writer celebrates God's mighty act in raising Jesus Christ from the dead. Christians share in this resurrection and so receive the power of a new life. This new life may involve suffering, but its keynote is joy.

*John 20.19–29*
The writer of John's Gospel records two appearances of the risen Jesus to the disciples: in the first, Jesus transfers his own mission to the disciples, and gives them the Spirit; in the second, the sceptical Thomas makes his confession of faith: Jesus is Lord. At both appearances, Jesus shows his wounds to the disciples: the writer wishes to make clear the fact that it really is the man, Jesus, and not a phantom.

### First year, evening

*Numbers 13.1–2, 17–33*
This story tells how spies go into the land of Canaan and report back to Moses and the people of Israel. It appears to be a mixture of two accounts, one of the exploration of the south only, the other of the whole country. The spies report that the land is fertile, but that the inhabitants are strong: the Nephilim are giants. The people are then warned that conquest will be difficult.

*II Corinthians 4.7–18*
In the course of defending his apostleship, Paul gives a graphic description of his own ministry, arguing that its very weakness is a sign of its authenticity, for it manifests the suffering and death of Jesus. This personal reflection leads Paul to a description of the Christian life as a dying and rising with Christ, and to a confession that Christian faith rests on the resurrection.

## The Bread of Life

### Second year, morning

*Exodus 16.4–15*
In response to the people's complaints in the wilderness, God tells Moses that he will send them food in the form of manna and quails. Manna is the honeydew excretion of certain insects which feed on tamarisk trees; quails migrate from Africa and are easy to catch as they fly over the Sinai peninsula. The story demonstrates the belief that God provided for the Israelites after they escaped from Egypt. It also contains a reflection of the later law of Sabbath observance.

*I Corinthians 15.53–58*
Paul indicates what he expects to happen at the end of all things, emphasizing the transformation of the physical body into a spiritual body. He asserts that sin is what makes death intolerable, but Christ is victorious over sin. For Paul, Jewish legalism gives sin its power. The quotations are from Isaiah and Hosea.

*John 6.35–40*
The feeding of the five thousand is followed by a discussion on the theme of the bread of life. Reference has been made to the manna given in the wilderness, and in contrast to the temporary nature of this food, the writer of John's Gospel portrays Jesus as the true bread of life. This claim is part of the writer's presentation of Jesus as the one who has come from God and who therefore acts on God's behalf.

### Second year, evening

*II Kings 7.1–16*
During the siege of Samaria by the Syrians, conditions in the city have become severe and food is expensive. The king blames Elisha

for this situation, because the prophet has argued that the people should resist the Syrians and trust God to save them. The prophet's response is to promise an end to the famine conditions and lower prices for food. The story tells how this happens.

*Acts 13.26–39*
In Paul's address in the synagogue at Pisidian Antioch, it is argued that in the resurrection God has overruled the Jewish rejection of Jesus. The speech is similar to those made by Peter in the earlier chapters of Acts, and is part of the story of how the Gospel was offered first to the Jews and then to the Gentiles.

ASB
Prefaces as above.

# Second Sunday after Easter

*The Emmaus Road*

## First year, morning

*Isaiah 25.6–9*
In a vision of the future, the prophet pictures a banquet on Mount
Zion where God is enthroned as Lord of the whole world. Such is
the triumph of his rule that even death will be abolished. This is a
rare conviction in the Jewish scriptures, and the early Christians
used this passage to describe the victory of the risen Christ over
death, the last enemy.

*Revelation 19.6–9*
The Christian prophet has been celebrating the fall of Rome; now
he rejoices that the kingdom of Christ is coming. In a passage
designed to encourage Christians in a time of persecution, he
pictures the triumph of Christ as a great marriage feast. This
description takes up a familiar image in Jewish scripture: that Israel
is the bride of God.

*Luke 24.13–35*   See Easter Day. Second year, evening.

## First year, evening

*Jeremiah 38.1–13*
In a biographical passage, Jeremiah recounts how he is put into an
empty water cistern. This action is brought about by the hatred of
the princes for a prophet who is undermining the strength of the
army by preaching doom and defeat. They are not prepared to kill
a man of God directly, but wish nevertheless to be rid of him, and it
is only through the intervention of a eunuch that the king orders his
rescue. The incident assures Jeremiah of God's continuing care.

*Romans 1.1–17*
Paul opens his letter to the Christians in Rome with an extended
greeting which includes an early confession of faith: Jesus is the
descendant of David, acknowledged to be Son of God and worshipped as Lord because of the resurrection. Paul concludes these

opening remarks with a brief outline of the gospel he preaches: he is offering salvation to Jew and Gentile alike, to anyone who responds in faith.

## *The Good Shepherd*

### Second year, morning

*Ezekiel 34.7–15*
The prophet attacks the rulers of Israel for failing in their duty to the people and promises that God will rule in their place. The leaders have been false shepherds. God alone is the true shepherd, and he will search out the lost sheep and feed them with good pasture. This prophecy probably arises out of the fall of Jerusalem to the Babylonians and the recognition of the failure of past leadership.

*I Peter 5.1–11*
The writer addresses the leaders of young churches threatened with persecution, and urges them to fulfil their pastoral role of caring for God's people. They are shepherds under Christ, the chief shepherd, and should follow his example. Their reward will be to share in Christ's glory, a reward given to all who suffer for his sake.

*John 10.7–18*
By presenting Jesus as the good shepherd, the writer of John's Gospel distinguishes him from the false messiahs and saviours who existed in the world at that time. The writer suggests ways in which his readers can distinguish the true from the false: it is the function of the true shepherd to care for the sheep, even at the cost of his own life.

### Second year, evening

*Isaiah 43.1–7*
Writing about the return of the exiles from Babylon, the prophet says that God will redeem them through the policy of Cyrus, King of Persia and Babylon. His policy was to return conquered peoples to their own lands. The prophet suggests that Cyrus is about to conquer the nations of North Africa as a compensation for his release of the Jews. To the prophet, the acknowledgement of one

God means that he is lord of history and controls the affairs of all peoples.

*John 21.1–14*
This is the story of the appearance of Jesus to some of his disciples, and the miraculous catch of fish. The story can be interpreted as an allegory about the community to which the writer belongs, the catch representing the number of Christian converts and the net the church in which they are held.

ASB
Prefaces as above.

# Third Sunday after Easter

*The Lakeside*

**First year, morning**

*Isaiah 61.11–13*
In these three verses, the prophet seeks to cheer his people with the good news that though the homeland to which they have returned from exile leaves much to be desired, God is still working for them.

*I Corinthians 15.1–11*
In the earliest written account of the resurrection, recorded to answer questions being asked in Corinth, Paul lists the appearances of Jesus. He includes within the list his own experience of the risen Christ, so testifying to his qualification to be an apostle, despite his personal unworthiness.

*John 21.1–14* See Second Sunday after Easter. Second year, evening.

**First year, evening**

*Nehemiah 2.1–18*
The Chronicler tells how Nehemiah gains the sympathy of Artaxerxes, king of Persia, for the condition of Jerusalem, and obtains permission to supervise repairs there. The story indicates the opposition this rebuilding brings from those in Samaria, referred to here as the land 'beyond the river'.

*II Corinthians 1.1–11*
Paul writes to the Corinthians in an attempt to heal the wounds caused by their rejection of his apostleship. He has experienced difficulties in his ministry in Asia and he speaks openly to them of his suffering there. These experiences, however, have led him to trust more in God: he speaks of the comfort he has received in his time of suffering, and of the deliverance God has brought to him.

*The Resurrection and the Life*

## Second year, morning

*I Kings 17.17–24*
Elijah has fled from Ahab the king and has been looked after by a Phoenician woman; but when the son of the house dies, the woman blames Elijah. This story tells how the boy is restored to life and illustrates the ancient belief that a man of God, such as Elijah, has an abundance of life, which can be breathed into a dead person. The story confirms that Elijah is a true prophet.

*Colossians 3.1–11*
Paul calls on the Colossian Christians to act in conformity with their baptism, in which they shared in the death and resurrection of Christ. The real glory, however, lies in the future. Paul then calls on these Christians to become, in practice, what they already are in Christ. He reminds them of the moral standards expected of them and reaffirms that God's renewal is for all men.

*John 11.17–27*
This reading is part of the story of the raising of Lazarus from the dead. Martha's faith that Jesus, if he had been present, would have saved her brother, becomes faith in Jesus as Messiah and Lord. The story of the raising of Lazarus is intended to illustrate and anticipate the life-giving power of the risen Christ.

## Second year, evening

*Isaiah 43.8–21*
The prophet speaks of God's revelation of himself, and suggests that it is not mere knowledge of God that is important, but rather, personal awareness of his saving power. The prophet believes that the redeeming activity of God is to be seen in the defeat of the Babylonians and the release of the Jews from exile. The God who brought the Israelites out of Egypt will rescue his people again.

*John 21.15–25*
The author of John's Gospel has written of the appearance of Jesus to his disciples while they were fishing; now he writes about two of the disciples in particular. First, Jesus reinstates Peter with a

*Third Sunday after Easter*

threefold question and commission: he is to be the shepherd and, as such, will lay down his life for his sheep. Then Peter asks about the beloved disciple, whose identity is not known, but whose role is to witness to the truth of this Gospel.

## ASB
*Isaiah 61.1–7*
In these verses, the prophet seeks to cheer his people with the good news that though the homeland to which they have returned from exile leaves much to be desired, God is still working for them. A time of prosperity and joy awaits them.

Other Prefaces as above.

# Fourth Sunday after Easter

*The Charge to Peter*

## First year, morning

*Isaiah 62.1–5*
After the exile, the prophet reassures the community in Jerusalem that he will constantly pray to God for the restoration of the city. His hope is that the people will enjoy a new relationship with God, and he expresses this hope in three vivid images: the new name, the crown and diadem, and the bridegroom and the bride.

*Revelation 3.14–22*
In the last of the seven letters to the churches, the author writes in emotional terms to the church at Laodicea, and condemns it for having no real enthusiasm. Possibly this prosperous community interpreted Christianity as little more than respectable morality; certainly, the people thought that they could manage very well on their own. They are therefore urged to repent. 'He who conquers' is the phrase used in the book of Revelation to describe the Christian martyr.

*John 21.15–22* See Third Sunday after Easter. Second year, evening.

## First year, evening

*Isaiah 2.1–5*
This prophecy expresses the hope that God will bring peace to the peoples of the world. The ideal of peace was firmly built into the covenant relationship of Israel with God: here it is extended to include all nations. In this vision of God's reign, peace is brought about by universal obedience to God's law.

*I Peter 1.10–21*
At the beginning of the letter, the writer has described Christian hope as founded on the resurrection of Christ. Now he speaks of the obligation this brings: God's people are called to be holy as God himself is holy. As an encouragement, the writer reminds his readers

*Fourth Sunday after Easter*

of Christ's work on their behalf. The image of ransom is derive
from the redeeming of a slave in the market-place and from God'
deliverance of the Israelites from Egypt.

## The Way, the Truth and the Life

### Second year, morning

*Proverbs 4.10–18*
The writer contrasts the way of the wise with the way of the wicked
comparing them to light and darkness. The reward for keeping th
law is long life and prosperity; the reward for wickedness is chao
and deep darkness. This doctrine of rewards and punishment
reflects the view of much of Jewish scripture, though it is challenge
by the book of Job and rejected by the preacher in Ecclesiastes.

*II Corinthians 4.11–18*
In the course of defending his apostleship, Paul has given a graphi
description of his own ministry, arguing that its very weakness is
sign of its authenticity, for it manifests the suffering and death o
Jesus. This personal reflection leads Paul to a description of th
Christian life as a dying and rising with Christ, and to a confessio
that Christian faith rests on the resurrection.

*John 14.1–11*
In this passage, Jesus strengthens his disciples for what is to come b
speaking to them of his departure and return, and of their ow
destiny, which is to be with him. Questions raised by two of th
disciples, Thomas and Philip, take them into deeper truth. For, i
response, Jesus is described not only as the way to God, but also a
the revelation of God himself.

### Second year, evening

*Habakkuk 3.1–13*
This passage is entitled 'A prayer of Habakkuk the prophet', but i
fact it is an imaginative description of God's march from Moun
Sinai to save his people. The poem describes God's victory in term
of ancient mythology: God, who created the world by overcomin
chaos and who led his people through the Red Sea, is still a God o
salvation. He will come once again to save his faithful people.

*Revelation 1.4–18*
The author opens his letters to the seven churches with an acknowledgment of the eternal nature of God and the glory of Jesus. He then describes in strange, symbolic language, his vision of the risen Christ, received while he was in a spiritual trance. The interpretation of the vision is that Christ is alive and will be alive for evermore. In him is to be found the key to life and death.


ASB
*II Corinthians 4.13–5.5*
In this passage Paul confesses that the Christian faith rests on the resurrection of Jesus. He looks forward to the glory of the resurrection life.

Other prefaces as above.

# Fifth Sunday after Easter

*Going to the Father*

## First year, morning

*Isaiah 51.1–6*
In a passage which calls on the exiled people of Israel to be awake
and listen to God, the prophet reminds the people of what God ha
done for them in the past. On this ground, he assures them that Goc
will again deliver his people, and through them extend his salvatior
to the whole world.

*I Corinthians 15.21–28*
Paul explains his belief in the resurrection through a comparisor
between Adam and Christ: just as Adam represents the old human
ity, so Christ is the beginning of the new humanity. Paul describe
the resurrection as taking place in stages: first Christ, then Christians
then all things handed over to God. The present time, betweer
Christ's resurrection and that of believers, is the reign of Christ
which will continue until his lordship is universally recognized.

*John 16.25–33*
In this passage, Jesus is conversing with his disciples at the Las
Supper, and he assures them that one day they will understand hi
message, just as one day they will pray with confidence to God in hi
name. But he then predicts that they will desert him when he i
arrested. For the writer of John's Gospel, their desertion reinforce
the belief that Jesus and the Father are one, for it is the Father wh
is present with Jesus in his hour of trial, not the disciples.

## First year, evening

*Isaiah 51.12–16*
Addressing the exiled people of Israel, the prophet presents God a
the creator and redeemer who will restore his people. The overthro
of Israel's enemies, whose temporary power is contrasted with th
eternal protection given by God, is therefore assured.

120

*Acts 24.1–21*
After his arrest at Jerusalem, Paul is tried before Felix, the Roman governor at Caesarea. The charge, made by a delegation led by the high priest, is that Paul is a danger to public order. Paul's defence is that he is a loyal Jew, though belonging to 'the Way', a term used of Christianity in the early days. He argues that the only charge that can properly be brought against him is that he believes in the resurrection.

## Second year, morning

*Deuteronomy 34.1–12*
The book of Deuteronomy closes with an account of the death of Moses on the edge of the promised land and Joshua's succession to the leadership of the people. This passage is an appreciation of Moses, a great spiritual and temporal leader, renowned as a prophet and a worker of miracles. He was the founder of the Hebrew nation.

*Romans 8.28–39*
Paul affirms his belief that God is in control of life, and this belief is so strong that he writes in terms of predestination. Those whom God has chosen are being made to be like Christ. It is Paul's experience of God's goodness and love which gives him confidence that not even the spiritual forces of the world, referred to in this passage as principalities and powers, can break the bond between God and his people.

*John 16.12–24*
The writer of John's Gospel reflects the experience of his own Christian community that the Spirit has led them into deeper truth concerning the relationship of Jesus with the Father. This relationship is expressed in terms of the going and coming of Jesus, probably referring to his death and resurrection. The image of childbirth is also used to illustrate the mixed sorrow and joy of these coming events.

## Second year, evening

*II Samuel 18.19–33*
Absalom, David's son, was trying to take over the land from his father. When David sent his army under Joab to fight Absalom, he

told his commanders to deal gently with his son. But after the battle Joab killed the unfortunate Absalom, who was caught by his hair in an oak tree. This dramatic passage describes how the news of the battle and the death of Absalom reaches king David.

*II Corinthians 5.1–15*
Paul speaks of the change which will come upon man after death. He sees the physical body as a temporary dwelling place, a tent which, after death, will be further clothed. For Paul, spiritual well-being is more important than physical condition; his aim therefore is not to preserve his life, but to please God. Though this passage has rather different language from that used in the section about the resurrection of the body in I Corinthians, central to them both is the belief that all life is controlled by God's love.

## ASB
## Year 1

*Hosea 6.1–6*
The opening verses of this passage express an act of penitence by the people and the firm belief that God is their only hope. The second part of the passage warns Israel against any insincere and shallow response to God. Only steadfast love will do.

## Years 1 and 2

Other Prefaces as above.

# Ascension Day

*The Ascension of Christ*

**First and second years, morning**

*Daniel 7.13–14*
The writer describes his vision of a divine figure who, after the overthrow of the kingdoms of this world, will rule for ever. Although there is no specific reference to the Messiah, this 'Son of man' is given a kingly role and the vision points to the coming of the kingdom of God.

*Acts 1.1–11*
The Acts of the Apostles opens with a description of the final resurrection appearance of Jesus, and his ascension follows, pictured here in physical terms. The cloud which receives Jesus is a sign of God's presence, and the two witnesses link this story with those of the transfiguration and the resurrection. All three testify to the glory of Jesus.

*Matthew 28.16–20*
This Gospel closes with an account of an appearance of the risen Jesus in glory on a mountain in Galilee. Christ, enthroned with power in heaven and earth, charges his disciples to take the gospel to the whole world, baptizing in the name of Father, Son and Spirit. The use of this threefold formula reflects the belief and practice of the early church. There follows a promise from Jesus to be with his disciples to the end of time.

**First year, evening**

*II Samuel 5.1–5*
This is the story of the Israelites recognizing David as their king after the death of Saul. He is acknowledged as a leader in battle and as a shepherd over his people. Before he is anointed, the accession of David to the throne is confirmed by a covenant made between him and the people.

*Ascension Day*

*Hebrews 2.5–18*
The writer of this letter, quoting from the Psalms, argues that Jesus is superior to the angels. He is also seeking to establish the superiority of the high-priesthood of Christ to the priesthood of the Jewish religion, in order to demonstrate the superiority of Christianity to Judaism. He therefore asserts that Christ had a real human nature: he suffered and was tempted. This humanity qualified him to be a sympathetic high-priest.

## Second year, evening

*Exodus 15.1–3, 11–18*
In a triumphal song, Moses and the people celebrate God's victory over the Egyptians. The song, which was later used in worship in the temple, celebrates the chief incident in the exodus, the most important event in the history of Israel. God is depicted as a mighty warrior who is able to overcome the enemy and control the forces of nature. Consequently other nations opposed to Israel are seized with fear.

*Hebrews 7.21–28*
The writer has been likening Jesus to Melchizedek, the priest whom even Abraham acknowledged as his superior. He goes on to argue that the priesthood of Jesus is superior to the Jewish priesthood, descended from Abraham. The passage concludes with a confession that Jesus is the eternal high priest, exalted in heaven, whose sacrifice is sufficient for all time.

## ASB
## Years 1 and 2

*Daniel 7.9–14*   See Sixth Sunday after Easter. First year, morning.

Other Prefaces as above.

# Sixth Sunday after Easter
(Sunday after Ascension Day)

*The Ascension of Christ*

### First year, morning

*Daniel 7.9–14*
In symbolic language, the writer describes his vision of God and the destruction of the kingdoms of this world. Then there appears a divine figure who will rule for ever. Although there is no specific reference to the Messiah, this 'Son of man' is given a kingly role and the vision points to the coming of the kingdom of God.

*Ephesians 1.15–23*
The writer thanks God for the faith of the Christians at Ephesus and prays that their knowledge of Christ may grow. The passage praises Christ, who has been exalted by God through the resurrection, and is now acknowledged as Lord within the church.

*Luke 24.44–53*
Luke closes his Gospel with the charge, given by the risen Christ to his disciples, that they should witness to his fulfilment of the Jewish scriptures. They are to preach repentance and forgiveness throughout the world, thus continuing the ministry of Jesus himself. The Gospel ends, as it began, in Jerusalem with the people waiting for the kingdom of God.

### First year, evening

*Jeremiah 10.1–10a*
The prophet Jeremiah ridicules the worship of idols and urges the Jewish exiles not to follow such heathen ways. He contrasts these man-made and lifeless images with the greatness and power of the one, true God.

*Revelation 5.1–14*
The writer has a vision of the heavenly worship of Christ, who is described, in language taken from Jewish scripture, as both the lion of Judah and the Lamb of God. The scene, expressed in symbolic

language, is of the whole heavenly court – indeed, the whole creation – worshipping the exalted Christ. This may well be intended as a contrast to the emperor-worship prevalent at the time and therefore as an encouragement to persecuted Christians to acknowledge Christ as king.

## Second year, morning

*II Kings 2.1–15*
This is the account of how Elisha succeeds Elijah. It records Elijah's farewell to various communities of prophets and Elisha's request for a double portion of his prophetic powers. This request is granted only because Elisha sees the vision of Elijah's departure: prophetic gifts could be handed on only to those worthy to receive them. The story is told as an introduction to a cycle of stories about Elisha, who hopes to be an even greater prophet than Elijah.

*Ephesians 4.1–8,11–13*
The writer calls for unity within the church, and identifies the ascended Christ as the source of the various gifts within the life of the Christian community. These gifts are to be used to equip God's people for their ministry, with the ultimate aim that all may grow in Christ.

*Luke 24.44–53*   See Sixth Sunday after Easter. First year, morning.

## Second year, evening

*Ezekiel 43.1–7a*
Ezekiel has a vision of God's return to the new temple in Jerusalem, which is to be a house where God's glory can be acknowledged for ever. From the temple, God will rule as king over his people.

*Hebrews 12.18–29*   See Sixth Sunday after Epiphany. Second year, morning.

ASB
Prefaces as above.

# Pentecost
(Whitsunday)

## *The Gift of the Spirit*

### First year, morning

*Joel 2.23–29*
The prophet Joel has warned the people that the unusually severe
plague of locusts which has come to the land may be a sign that the
day of judgment is near. Now he records God's response to the
people's repentance: a good harvest, with abundant food and drink,
a pledge that the plague will not recur and a promise that his spirit
will be given to all.

*Acts 2.1–11*
Using images from the Old Testament, the writer describes the
coming of the Spirit to the apostles gathered together for the feast
of Pentecost, the festival at which Jews celebrated the giving of the
law. The story recounts how the giving of the Spirit enables the
apostles to preach to men of all nations. This is appropriate at the
start of the Acts of the Apostles, for the book is the story of the
spread of the gospel to the whole known world, under the power of
the Spirit.

*John 14.15–27*
The writer records Jesus's promise that God will give the Spirit to
the disciples. The Spirit will remind them of the teaching of Jesus,
and will be with them for ever. It is likely that the church to which
the writer belonged had already experienced the Spirit in this way.

### First year, evening

*Exodus 19.16–25*   See Sixth Sunday after Epiphany. Second year,
morning.

*Acts 4.23–37*
The writer tells how Peter and John, released by the Jewish
authorities, return to their fellow Christians and together they pray
to God. The prayer is probably typical of early Christian worship

*Pentecost*

and is modelled on prayers found in Jewish scripture, including a quotation from Psalm 2. It recalls God's mighty wonders in the past and calls for them to be repeated in the life of the church. The passage concludes with an account of the sharing of possessions in the early Christian community in Jerusalem.


## Second year, morning

*Joel 2.28–32*
The prophet Joel has warned the people that the unusually severe plague of locusts which has come to the land may be a sign that the day of judgment is near. Now he speaks of two features of this coming judgment: the gift of God's spirit to all, and supernatural changes in the physical world, believed to be portents of God's judgment.

*Acts 2.1–11*   See First year, morning.

*John 14.15–27*   See First year, morning.


## Second year, evening

*Zechariah 4.1–10*
The prophet describes his vision of a seven-branched candlestick and two olive trees. These represent the eyes of God over the whole world and the two agents of God, Zerubbabel and Joshua, leaders of the Jerusalem community after the exile. The passage stresses Zerubbabel's role in rebuilding the temple, and probably reflects an attempt to rouse enthusiasm for the rebuilding project at a time of discouragement.

*I Corinthians 3.16–23*
Paul speaks of the church as a temple : a holy place where the Spirit of God dwells. He warns his opponents not to destroy the church he has built up at Corinth. He attacks their pretension to wisdom and reminds his readers that, in the end, they all belong to Christ and God. There is therefore no occasion for any of the leaders at Corinth to boast about their achievements.

# ASB
**Years 1 and 2**

*Genesis 11.1–9*
This ancient story of the tower of Babel is an explanation of the diversity of human language. The desire of the builders to reach heaven with their tower implies a rejection of God's rule and leads to their dispersal around the world. God's judgment on the people is the disintegration of the unity which he brought about at the creation.

*Exodus 19.16–25*  See Sixth Sunday after Epiphany. Second year, morning.

*Acts 2.1–11*  Preface as above.

*Acts 2.1–21*
Using images from the Old Testament, the writer describes the coming of the Spirit to the apostles gathered together for the feast of Pentecost, the festival at which Jews celebrated the giving of the law. The story recounts how the giving of the Spirit enables the apostles to preach to men of all nations. This is appropriate at the start of the Acts of the Apostles, for the book is the story of the spread of the gospel to the whole known world, under the power of the Spirit. The passage concludes with the opening section of a sermon by Peter.

*John 14.15–26*  Preface as above.

*John 20.19–23*
This passage records an appearance of the risen Jesus to the disciples. He shows them his wounds: the writer wishes to make clear the fact that it really is the man, Jesus, and not a phantom. Jesus then transfers his own mission to them and gives them the Spirit.

# Trinity Sunday
(First Sunday after Pentecost)

## The Riches of God

### First year, morning

*Isaiah 6.1–8*
Isaiah gives an account of his call to be a prophet during a service in the temple. The ritual and the rising incense lead him to a vision of God's glory. His reaction is one of fear, for it is not possible to see God and live. The burning coal symbolizes both the cleansing of his sin and the purifying of the word he is to preach.

*Ephesians 1.3–14*
After his opening greeting, the writer plunges into a hymn of praise for what God has done for those who are in Christ, and he describes God's plan for the unity of all things. This plan includes the Gentiles, for they also are to know God's love in Christ and to receive the Holy Spirit.

*John 14.8–17*
As a response to Philip's demand to see the Father, the writer of John's Gospel shows how Jesus reveals the Father: he always speaks and acts in obedience to him. The Spirit, like the Son, is not recognized by the world, but is known by believers as a further witness to God. The passage therefore indicates the close relationship between Father, Son and Spirit: the Son came to witness to the Father, the Spirit keeps alive this witness within the church.

### First year, evening

*Isaiah 40.12–17*
As preparation for the announcement that God will save his people from exile, the prophet gives his reasons for believing in the sovereign power of God the creator. He who made the world is well able to deal with the nations, for they are as nothing before him.

*John 5.17–27*
After the healing of the invalid at the pool in Jerusalem, the Jewish opponents of Jesus quarrel with him, because he has broken the Sabbath. The argument leads to an explanation of the relationship between Jesus and the Father. The writer has two themes: Jesus is the divine Son of God; Jesus is dependent upon and obedient to the Father. As a result, Jesus can raise the dead and act as judge of all the earth.

## *The Church's Message*

### Second year, morning

*Deuteronomy 6.4–9*
This passage, known as the Shema, contains the central proclamation of the Jewish faith: there is one, true God. It also describes man's proper response to God: total love. Such is the importance of this prayer that it must not only be taught to children, but also be bound on the foreheads of the people. This instruction may at first have been intended metaphorically, but later was taken literally. The Shema and other passages, written on small scrolls, were either worn by the person or fastened to his house, as here directed.

*Acts 2.22–24, 32–36*
Peter, filled with new power, attacks the Jews for killing Jesus, an action which he contrasts with the way God has glorified Jesus in the resurrection. In this sermon, Peter presents his belief about Jesus in terms reminiscent of the central Jewish prayer, the Shema. He also uses, in the style of Jewish argument, quotations from the Psalms. Finally, he calls upon the Jews to accept Jesus as Lord.

*Matthew 11.25–30*
This passage begins with a prayer of Jesus. He gives thanks for the divine revelation. Only the Father can reveal the true identity of Jesus; only Jesus, the Son, can reveal God the Father. In the context of this special relationship with God, Jesus invites men to come to him, and offers them release from the yoke of the law. Thus the writer of the Gospel presents the way of Jesus as an alternative to the Judaism of his day.

*Trinity Sunday*

**Second year, evening**

*Jeremiah 18.1–10*
A visit to the potter's house gives Jeremiah a deep insight into the future of his people. He learns that God is able to remake the people of Israel just as the potter can break and remould the clay. In this prophecy there is both judgment and promise.

*I Timothy 6.12–16*
This passage is a challenge to Timothy to hold fast the faith and to live a good life. Reference is made to Timothy's good confession, probably at his baptism, possibly at his ordination, a confession following the example of Jesus before Pontius Pilate. The substance of Timothy's confession was probably the early creed, Jesus is Lord.


ASB
Prefaces as above for First year.

# Second Sunday after Pentecost
(Trinity 1)

*The People of God*

### First year, morning

*Exodus 19.1–6*
The Israelites come to Mount Sinai, where the terms of God's covenant with them are set out. God, for his part, claims the people as his own possession and will protect them; the Israelites, for their part, must obey God's law. The Israelite nation is then described as a kingdom of priests. This term signifies that the whole people have the privilege of approaching God and the responsibility of bringing other nations to him.

*1 Peter 2.1–10*
The writer expresses his belief that coming to Christ means joining the community which belongs to Christ. He sees this community as the new Israel, whose life is to be one of worship and witness. The image of the stone, used to describe Christ and to indicate the nature of the church, is derived from various passages in Jewish scripture. The quotations given here show how, for some, the stone is precious and, for others, a cause of stumbling.

*John 15.1–5*
The familiar Jewish image of the vine is here used to claim that Jesus, not Israel, is the true vine. The Christian community becomes the true people of God through its close relationship with him.

### First year, evening

*Ezekiel 37.15–23*
Ezekiel is commanded to join together two sticks to symbolize and bring about the reunion of the two kingdoms, Judah and Israel, under one king. In their restored unity the Jewish people will be faithful to God.

*Second Sunday after Pentecost*

*Ephesians 2.11–22*
This passage asserts that God's grace extends to Gentiles as well as
to Jews. It explains how the Gentiles have become part of the new
Israel: Christ has destroyed all that divided Jew and Gentile, and
the new unity they experience is derived entirely from him. The
passage concludes with a picture of the church as a building in which
Christ is the cornerstone that holds the structure together.


## The Church's Unity and Fellowship

### Second year, morning

*II Samuel 7.4–16*
David has consulted Nathan, the prophet, about the building of a
temple and has been encouraged by him to proceed. But in this
passage Nathan is told that the temple will be built by David's son.
These verses include the first mention of what was to become a
fundamental promise for both Jews and Christians: the house and
kingdom of David will be for ever.

*Acts 2.37–47*
In response to Peter's speech at Pentecost, the people express
repentance by being baptized in the name of Jesus. Their baptism is
accompanied by the gift of the Spirit, and these two are seen as the
marks of belonging to the church. The passage concludes with a
summary of the life of the early Christian community.

*Luke 14.15–24*
The occasion for the parable of the great supper is a meal at the
house of one of the leading Pharisees. Jesus has just urged his
fellow-guests not to invite friends to their banquets, but those in
need. The parable shows that the kingdom of God is a present
reality, calling for an immediate response. No one is excluded from
it, Jew or Gentile, save by his or her own choice. The kingdom of
God was frequently pictured as a banquet, and the image is used
here to indicate different responses to the call of Jesus.


### Second year, evening

*Deuteronomy 30.1–10*
This passage contains God's promise to restore the children of Israel
to their own land and to give them prosperity. But the promise

134

conditional on their repentance: the people must be faithful to God
and keep his law. Although written in the context of Moses's
leadership of the children of Israel in the wilderness, this passage is
typical of Israel's continuous understanding of her covenant relationship with God.

*Matthew 18.10–20*
Matthew uses the parable of the lost sheep to illustrate God's
continuing care for Christians who have lapsed. The parable leads
into a description of how discipline is to be exercised within the life
of the church. The concluding promise of the presence of Christ
assures church leaders that they have his authority to exercise
discipline.

ASB
Prefaces as above.

# Third Sunday after Pentecost
(Trinity 2)

*The Life of the Baptized*

**First year, morning**

*Deuteronomy 6.17–25*
This passage argues that the justification of the law is to be found in
the story of Israel's deliverance from Egypt. It is through his law
that God rules and preserves his people; therefore, only through
obedience to those laws can the life of the people be secure. Part of
the passage is in the form of an early catechism, through which the
faith and duty of the Israelites was handed down from one generation
to another.

*Romans 6.1–11*
Paul rejects the false teaching that Christians are allowed to sin in
order to increase the action of God's grace. His reply draws attention
to what happens in Christian baptism, which he describes as a dying
and rising with Christ.

*John 15.6–11*
In the metaphor of the vine, the life of the disciples was shown to be
dependent on Christ, who is the true vine. The writer now reinforces
his message with a call for Christians to keep the commandments of
Jesus. Their response to God's love should be one of joyful
obedience.

**First year, evening**

*Proverbs 16.18–32*
In this collection of ancient proverbs, the attitude of the wise is
contrasted with that of the foolish, in a manner typical of the book
of Proverbs. The general theme of the passage is that of right and
wise conduct, though each proverb stands on its own and the
connection of thought is not precise.

*Matthew 5.38–48*

This passage records two contrasts between the demand of the law and the response ideally required of a Christian disciple. Both illustrate the writer's claim that the law has been fulfilled in Christ. It is better to be generous than to retaliate; it is more rewarding to love an enemy than a friend.


*The Church's Confidence in Christ*

## Second year, morning

*Deuteronomy 8.11–20*

The writer urges the people not to forget, in their prosperity, what God has done for them in the past. They must reject the temptation to attribute their success either to themselves or to false gods.

*Acts 4.5–12*

After Peter and John had healed a lame man at the gate of the temple, they were arrested for preaching about Jesus. In this passage, Peter addresses the court, and takes the opportunity of proclaiming the power of the risen Christ. The story illustrates how the early Christians saw persecution as an opportunity for witness and preaching.

*Luke 8.41–55*

This passage contains the stories of the healing of a woman with a haemorrhage, and the raising of Jairus's daughter. In both incidents, great emphasis is placed on faith: the woman was healed because of her faith; Jairus is urged to have faith. The stories are recorded by Luke to encourage Christians to have confidence in the power of Christ.


## Second year, evening

*Proverbs 22.1–12*

In this collection of ancient proverbs, the attitude of the wise is contrasted with that of the foolish in a manner typical of the book of Proverbs. The general theme of the passage is that of right and wise conduct, though each proverb stands on its own and the connection of thought is not precise.

*Third Sunday after Pentecost*

*I Corinthians 1.1–17*
Paul opens this letter with a greeting and a thanksgiving. He then makes an appeal for unity and an end to dissension among the Corinthians. In this context, he affirms that his only interest is to preach the message of the cross of Christ. For Paul, Christ is the wisdom of God and any display of human wisdom is to be set aside. Christ's leadership alone is to be acknowledged.

## ASB
## Year 1

*Romans 6.3–11*
Paul has rejected the false teaching that Christians are allowed to sin in order to increase the action of God's grace. He now replies, drawing attention to what happens in Christian baptism: it is a dying and rising with Christ.

## Years 1 and 2

Other Prefaces as above.

# Fourth Sunday after Pentecost
(Trinity 3)

*The Freedom of the Sons of God*

**First year, morning**

*Deuteronomy 7.6–9a*
The writer explains why the people of Israel are God's chosen people. He then asserts that God will always be faithful to the covenant which he has made with Israel.

*Galatians 3.26–4.7*
Paul contends that the unity of baptized Christians in Christ is of more significance than divisions of race, class or sex. It is through the presence of the Spirit of Christ, superseding the Jewish law, that Christians are able to call God Father, as Jesus did.

*John 15.12–15*
The writer of John's Gospel stresses the need for the Christian life to be marked by sacrificial love. Such love is the characteristic of those who are no longer servants but friends of Christ.

**First year, evening**

*Jeremiah 20.7–13*
Jeremiah writes of his despondency because of a compulsion from God to preach doom at a time of comparative peace. He is rejected by his fellow countrymen, who not only refuse to hear his message but also plot against him. However, his initial feeling that God has deceived him is replaced by a firm belief in divine protection.

*John 8.21–36*
The writer of John's Gospel contrasts those who reject Jesus and do not understand his claim with those who believe in him. The unbelievers will die in their sins, but the believers are promised freedom from theirs.

*Fourth Sunday after Pentecost*

*The Church's Mission to the Individual*

## Second year, morning

*Joshua 24.14–25*
The writer records the second farewell address of Joshua and the response of the people. Joshua urges the Israelites to think carefully about their choice between the God who brought them out of Egypt into the promised land and the local gods. The passage concludes with an account of the covenant made at Shechem.

*Acts 8.26–38*
This is the account of the conversion and baptism of the Ethiopian eunuch through the ministry of Philip. The story is used to point to the imminent spread of the gospel among the Gentiles and therefore serves as an introduction to the ministry of Paul, the chief character in the rest of the book of Acts.

*Luke 15.1–10*
Luke sets the parables of the lost sheep and the lost coin in the context of the criticism that Jesus spends his time with sinners. 'Sinners' here means the ordinary people who do not observe the law, as strictly interpreted by the Pharisees. In Luke's mind, the contrast is probably between Israel, the chosen people, and the Gentiles. The two parables, therefore, illustrate not only Jesus's concern for individuals who are lost, but also the spread of the gospel beyond Judaism.

## Second year, evening

*Ezekiel 18.1–4, 19–23*
Ezekiel rejects a familiar proverb, which suggested that the plight of the exiles was a punishment for the sins of their ancestors. Instead, he affirms God's interest in each individual and the responsibility of each person for his own life. According to Ezekiel, the righteous person and the penitent will both live, but the unrepentant sinner will die.

*John 4.5–26*
This passage describes the encounter between Jesus and the woman of Samaria at Jacob's well. The Samaritans were the descendants of

the people of the northern kingdom of Israel who were not taken
into exile. They subsequently intermarried with other races and
were despised by the Jews for their racial impurity. The story is told
to show that, just as Jesus is the fulfilment of Judaism, so also he
fulfils the hopes of the Samaritans.

## ASB
## Year 1

*Deuteronomy 7.6–11*
The writer explains why the people of Israel are God's chosen
people. He then asserts that God will always be faithful to the
covenant which he has made with Israel. But the enemies of God
will be destroyed.

*Galatians 3.23–4.7*
Paul points out that the law is superseded by the coming of Christ.
He then contends that the unity of baptized Christians in Christ is of
more significance than divisions of race, class or sex. It is through
the presence of the Spirit of Christ that Christians are able to call
God Father, as Jesus did.

*John 15.12–17*
The writer of John's Gospel stresses the need for the Christian life
to be marked by sacrificial love. Such love is the characteristic of
those who are no longer servants but friends of Christ, chosen and
appointed by him.

## Year 2

*Isaiah 63.7–14*
The prophet proclaims the love of God for his people, demonstrated
by the way in which he has delivered them from Egypt.

*Acts 8.26–38*   Preface as above.

*Luke 15.1–10*   Preface as above.

# Fifth Sunday after Pentecost
(Trinity 4)

## The New Law

### First year, morning

*Exodus 20.1–17*
This passage contains the ten commandments. They are prefaced by a reminder of God's deliverance of the Israelites from Egypt, and the obedience urged in the commandments themselves is a response to that saving action. The commandments are not a detailed code of law but a statement of basic obligations to God and to other people.

*Ephesians 5.1–10*
The writer has outlined the nature of the new life given in Christ. Now he draws out its moral implications, contrasting the behaviour required of a Christian with the immorality prevalent in society. This new life is an imitation of God, whose love was shown in Jesus Christ.

*Matthew 19.16–26*
Matthew tells the story of a rich young man, whose quest for perfection is frustrated by his attachment to his possessions. It is argued that wealth is a risk to discipleship, reflecting an element in Jewish piety which tended to identify the rich with the ungodly.

### First year, evening

*Deuteronomy 6.4–15*
The first part of this passage, known as the Shema, contains the central proclamation of the Jewish faith: there is one true God. It also describes man's proper response to God: total love. In the second part of the passage, the people are warned not to let the riches of life in Canaan lead them to forget God. The writer fears that prosperity will lead to idolatry.

*Matthew 7.1–12*
The first part of this passage from the Sermon on the Mount contains instructions for the Christian life. The second part speaks of the

confidence with which the disciple is able to approach God. The final verse 13 is the golden rule, which the writer acknowledges to be a summary of the best of Old Testament religion.

## The Church's Mission to All Men

### Second year, morning

#### Ruth 1.8–17,22

This passage introduces the story of the book of Ruth: Ruth, the Moabitess, returns with her mother-in-law to the land of Israel; there she marries Boaz, and the child born to them is ancestor to David. At the time the book was written, there were great pressures for the Jewish community to become exclusive, but the writer has used a beautiful and ancient story to suggest that the Jewish people have a message which must be shared with those who are not Jews.

#### Acts 11.4–18

Peter tells the Jerusalem church of his vision at Joppa, as a result of which he preached to Gentiles. The authorities at Jerusalem come to recognize that Peter's action was right. The episode is part of the account in the book of Acts of the extension of the church's mission to the Gentiles.

#### Luke 17.11–19

Luke tells how the healing power of Jesus is extended to a group of lepers, only one of whom returns to thank him. He is a Samaritan, despised by the Jews. The story anticipates the mission of the church to Samaritans and Gentiles, and illustrates how this extension is in accord with the ministry of Jesus.

### Second year, evening

#### Jonah 3.1–10

In this passage, the people of Nineveh repent when Jonah preaches judgment. The book of Jonah shows how God's mercy extends even to the people of this evil city, and the final chapter tells how God tries to convince the disgruntled prophet that such mercy is entirely right. The book as a whole is a plea to the Jews, in the form of a story, that they should welcome non-Israelites who turn to God in repentance.

*Fifth Sunday after Pentecost*

*John 4.27–42*
This passage concludes the account of Jesus talking with the Samaritan woman at Jacob's well. Many Samaritans believe in Jesus as a result of the woman's testimony: they are a harvest of converts. It is in this context that the writer of John's Gospel affirms that Jesus is the Saviour of all men.

ASB
**Year 1**

Prefaces as above.

**Year 2**

*Ruth 1.8–17, 22*   Preface as above.

*Acts 11.4–18*   Preface as above.

*Luke 10.1–12*
Luke describes the mission of the seventy followers of Jesus and the instructions given to them for their work. Their central message is the nearness of the kingdom of God. This story, found only in Luke's Gospel, is seen by the writer as an anticipation of the disciples' mission to the whole world after the resurrection.

# Sixth Sunday after Pentecost
(Trinity 5)

---

*The New Man*

### First year, morning

*Exodus 24.3–11*
This passage contains two accounts, originally independent, of the sealing of the covenant between God and his people. The first records the covenant being confirmed by sacrifice and the sprinkling of blood. The second speaks of a meal at which the covenant was confirmed by Moses and the elders of Israel, following their vision of God.

*Colossians 3.12–17*
Paul continues his practical application of belief in the resurrection. He has urged the Colossians to put an end to immoral behaviour; now he tells them to adopt a new nature, and points to Christ as the example they should follow. The image of 'putting on' is probably related to the practice of baptism, where a new garment was put on as a symbol of new life.

*Luke 15.11–32*
Luke tells the story of two sons, one of whom is righteous, the other prodigal. The story illustrates many aspects of the teaching of Jesus, but particularly the contrast between God's welcome to those who repent and the refusal of the self-righteous to accept them. Perhaps the writer intends the two sons to represent the righteous in Israel and the outcast but repentant Gentiles, to whom the gospel is now offered.

### First year, evening

*Malachi 3.13–18*
The prophet records the reaction of whose who see men despising God and receiving no punishment. He tells the faithful worshippers that at the day of judgment they will receive God's special blessing. The prophecy belongs to a time shortly after the return of the people

from exile, before the reforms of Ezra and Nehemiah had brough
order to the community at Jerusalem.

*Luke 6.17–26*
Luke opens his account of this sermon, preached by Jesus, with fou
blessings and four corresponding woes. The blessings are thos
which will be given to the disciples of Jesus. The woes, found onl
in Luke's Gospel, are not addressed to the disciples, but describ
the condition of those who reject the kingdom of God.

## Second year, morning

*Micah 6.1–8*
Micah pictures a law-court scene in which God reminds the people
of what he has done for them in the past and argues that they have
not fulfilled their obligations in return. The passage is part of the
prophet's attack upon the moral corruption of eighth-century Israe
and Judah. It concludes with a statement of what God demands from
his people: not sacrifices, but rather a new life of justice, kindnes
and humility. This concluding verse is a summary of the practica
religion advocated by the prophets.

*Ephesians 4.17–32*
The writer describes the character of the new life in Christ in term
of practical conduct. The image of 'putting on' is probably related to
the early Christian practice of baptism, where a new garment wa
put on as a symbol of new life.

*Mark 10.46–52*
This is the story of the healing of blind Bartimaeus. It shows the
compassion of Jesus in contrast to the indifference of others present
The story is used to illustrate the new life available to those who are
persistent in calling on Jesus.

## Second year, evening

*Proverbs 18.10–24*
This collection of ancient proverbs refers, among other things, to
the insecurity of worldly success and suggests alternative values
such as humility, wisdom and friendship.

*I John 2.7–17*

The writer contrasts hatred and darkness with love and light. It is typical of this letter to warn against worldiness. The writer regards it as foolishnesss to prefer the things of the world, which are dying, to the things of God, which are eternal.


ASB
Prefaces as above.

# Seventh Sunday after Pentecost
(Trinity 6)

*The More Excellent Way*

### First year, morning

*Hosea 11.1–9*
More than any other prophet, Hosea sees the relationship between God and Israel as that of a loving father and his son. In this passage God speaks of his care of Israel in the past and expresses his sorrow that his people still turn from him and put their trust in foreign nations. Yet God in his love cannot bring himself to punish them nor ever to let them go.

*I Corinthians 13.1–13*
In this hymn on the nature of love, Paul maintains that, without love, other gifts of the Spirit and acts of sacrifice are valueless. He lists the characteristics of love. It is the mark of Christian maturity. It is the greatest gift.

*Matthew 18.21–35*
Matthew stresses the importance of forgiveness within the Christian community, using as illustrations a conversation between Peter and Jesus and the parable of the unmerciful servant. Two aspects of forgiveness emerge: first, no limits can be set to it; second, those who do not practise it are in no position to claim the forgiveness of God.

### First year, evening

*I Samuel 24.1–17*
This is the story of how David spares the life of Saul, the king, at a time when David is outlawed and Saul is seeking to capture him. David's refusal to injure Saul is out of respect for the anointed king and fear of God's judgment. The consequence of this incident is that Saul gives David his blessing and assures him that he will succeed to the throne.

148

*Luke 6.27–36*
In a continuation of Jesus' sermon to the disciples, Luke describes the character of those who accept the kingdom of God. Love is the chief mark of discipleship, love which extends beyond friends to enemies. Luke commends merciful and forgiving love as the quality of God himself.

## Second year, morning

*Deuteronomy 10.12–11.1*
The writer describes Israel's duty to God: it is a life directed towards God in reverence, love and obedience. This passage is a summary of priestly teaching at its best.

*Romans 8.1–11*
Paul here describes the life of those who belong to Christ as a life of freedom under the Spirit. He distinguishes between those who live to please themselves and exclude God – this is the meaning of living 'according to the flesh' – and those who live to please God and are in union with Christ. Paul clearly believes that life with God will prove even stronger than physical death. He makes no attempt to distinguish between Christ and the Spirit: both are the real presence of God.

*Mark 12.28–34*
Mark records a conversation between Jesus and a scribe, in which Jesus says that to love God and to love one's neighbour are the greatest commandments. In this reply, Jesus combines the basic Jewish law in Deuteronomy, to love God, with the command in the book of Leviticus, to love one's neighbour. This may have been the first time such a combination was made. Certainly it influenced the teaching of the early church.

## Second year, evening

*Deuteronomy 24.10–22*
The writer records a series of laws which are intended to help the poor and others who suffer injustice. At their root lies the memory that the Israelites themselves were once slaves in Egypt.

*Seventh Sunday after Pentecost*

*I John 3.13–24*
The writer reminds his community of the need for love as the mark
of a disciple. The life of Jesus is the true pattern, and it is his
commandment to love which expresses man's proper response to
God.

## ASB
**Year 1**

*Hosea 11.1–9*  Preface as above.

*I Corinthians 12.27 – 13 end*
Paul writes of the gifts of the Spirit. Then follows a hymn on the
nature of love. In it Paul maintains that, without love, other gifts of
the Spirit and acts of sacrifice are valueless. He lists the characteristics of love. It is the mark of Christian maturity. It is the greatest
gift.

*Matthew 18.21 – end*   Preface as above.

**Year 2**

Prefaces as above.

# Eighth Sunday after Pentecost
(Trinity 7)

## The Fruit of the Spirit

### First year, morning

*Ezekiel 36.24–28*
Speaking to the Jews in exile, Ezekiel promises that they will be transformed when they return to their own land. They will be inwardly cleansed and renewed. This transformation will enable them to be obedient, and to renew their covenant relationship with God.

*Galatians 5.16–25*
Paul contrasts the works of the flesh with the fruit of the Spirit. 'The flesh' does not refer to the physical body alone, but to all self-centredness which shuts out God. Some of the works of the flesh are spiritual sins. In contrast, the good life is marked by the fruit of the Spirit.

*John 15.16–27*
The writer of John's Gospel contrasts the characteristic of the world, which is hatred, with the characteristic of the Christian disciple, which is love. By 'the world' he means those who have rejected God as he has revealed himself in Christ. He reminds Christians that they must expect the world to hate them, for this is how it treated Christ. Such treatment is condemned as a rejection of God.

### First year, evening

*Isaiah 32.14–18*
The prophet shares his vision of the radical change which will come upon the land and its people when the spirit of God is poured out upon them. This description of the ideal order includes both a transformation of nature and the establishment of justice and peace among the people.

*Eighth Sunday after Pentecost*

*Luke 6.37–49*
In a continuation of the sermon of Jesus to his disciples, Luke describes the life of those who belong to the kingdom of God. Much of the material seems directed to those in the early church who were concerned with pastoral care and preaching; it includes a warning against false discipleship and a reminder that only a true disciple can expect to have a fruitful ministry.


## Second year, morning

*Ezekiel 37.1–14*
Ezekiel records his vision of the valley of dry bones, the remains of men killed long ago in battle. Although it seems to him impossible that such men could live again, since all vitality has gone from them, the prophet obeys God's command to bring them back to life. The bones represent Israel. She is to rise from her death in exile and live again through the transforming work of God's spirit.

*I Corinthians 12.4–13*
Paul reminds the Corinthian Christians of the variety of gifts of the Spirit present within the life of the church. He stresses that the Spirit is the source of all these gifts, each of which is a contribution to the Christian community. The unity of the church, which the apostle is anxious to emphasize to the quarrelsome Corinthians, is illustrated by a comparison between the church and the human body.

*Luke 6.27–38*   See Seventh Sunday after Pentecost. First year, evening.


## Second year, evening

*Numbers 11.16–17, 24–29*
The writer tells how God responds to Moses's call for help by appointing elders to assist him in his work. At their appointment, the elders receive the spirit of prophecy, though only for a short time. Two of them, however, continue to prophesy. Joshua is alarmed lest these two will be thought to rival Moses and undermine his leadership, but Moses does not share his fear.

Acts 8.14–25

The writer tells of the visit of Peter and John to Samaria. They are sent from Jerusalem to set the seal of apostolic approval on the mission of Philip. Their prayer for the gift of the Spirit to come upon the Christians in Samaria prompts Simon Magus, a magician, to offer payment for this gift. Possibly he was impressed by speaking with tongues or some other physical sign associated with the Spirit.

ASB
Prefaces as above.

# Ninth Sunday after Pentecost
(Trinity 8)

## The Whole Armour of God

### First year, morning

*Joshua 1.1–9*
The book of Joshua introduces the story of the conquest of the land
of Canaan with this account of Joshua's commission. He is to succeed
Moses as leader of Israel and is promised God's presence. He is
urged to keep the law and told that obedience to it will assure success
and prosperity.

*Ephesians 6.10–18a*
The writer uses the image of warfare to describe the relation between
good and evil. He depicts the Christian as a soldier in full armour
resisting the powers of evil and remaining faithful in his discipleship.

*John 17.11–19*
In this passage Jesus prays that when the disciples are left alone
after his departure they may be protected from the world, to which
they do not really belong. By 'the world' the writer means human
society which has rejected Christ and stands in opposition to God.

### First year, evening

*II Samuel 23.8–17*
This is the story of how three of David's greatest soldiers break
through the Philistine lines at Bethlehem to bring water to David
from his home well. David attaches great value to their courage.
Possibly this incident took place when David was outlawed under
the rule of Saul, or at a time during David's reign when the Philistines
were in a strong position.

*Acts 19.23–41*
The writer records a riot against Paul at Ephesus. The disorder is
stirred up by a silversmith who has lost some of his trade when, as a
result of Paul's preaching, the people turn away from the worship of
Artemis. Artemis was an Asian goddess of fertility whose worship
was centred in Ephesus.

## Second year, morning

*I Samuel 17.37–50*
This is the story of how David, a young shepherd, accepts the challenge of the Philistine champion, Goliath, and kills him with a stone from his sling. Important elements in the story are the fearless bravery of David and his trust in God. The story introduces David to life at court and is a preface to accounts of his later relations with the king.

*II Corinthians 6.3–10*
Paul contends that his apostolic ministry is genuine because of the sufferings he has endured for Christ. In a deeply emotional and poetic passage, he argues that the only weapons he has used in his fight to secure his apostleship have been those proper to the Christian life. Some at Corinth may have despised his ministry, but he argues that it has been for the enrichment of the church.

*Mark 9.14–29*
Mark tells of the return of Jesus with three of his disciples after the transfiguration to find that the other disciples have failed to heal an epileptic boy. Then follows a graphic account of how Jesus heals the boy. The narrative stresses the need for faith and prayer.

## Second year, evening

*II Samuel 1.17–27*
This lamentation expresses David's deep sorrow when news is brought of the deaths of Saul and Jonathan in a battle against the Philistines. As a result of their deaths, David becomes king over Judah, and this incident, which illustrates the deep love he felt for Jonathan, marks the beginning of his reign.

*I Thessalonians 5.8–24*
Paul urges Christians to put on the armour of faith, hope and love. Furthermore, they are to encourage one another in the Christian life. The letter concludes with a prayer for their salvation.

## ASB
Prefaces as above.

# Tenth Sunday after Pentecost
(Trinity 9)

*The Mind of Christ*

**First year, morning**

*Job 42.1–6*
This passage concludes the poetic section of the book of Job and contains Job's response to God. Its attitude of submission is in marked contrast to the earlier defiance with which Job demanded justice for himself. But, since then, he has been confronted with God and a recital of God's mighty works. His present repentance is a result of that experience.

*Philippians 2.1–13*
Paul invites the Christians at Philippi to cultivate within their fellowship a quality of life based on communion with Christ. He recalls the example of Christ, particularly his humility and self-denial for the sake of others. Part of this passage is thought to be an early Christian hymn on the theme of the humiliation and exaltation of Christ. The last two verses indicate that salvation is both God's work and ours.

*John 13.1–15*   See Maundy Thursday. First year.

**First year, evening**

*II Samuel 9.1–13*
The writer tells how king David welcomes Jonathan's son at court and makes him a retainer in his household. In addition to being 'for Jonathan's sake', this action may have been to prevent reprisals against a member of Saul's family and to guard against any rebellion which might centre on Jonathan's son. This story is part of the court history of David.

*Mark 9.33–50*
Mark has gathered together material which illustrates Jesus's understanding of true greatness: it consists of humility, openness,

tolerance and single-mindedness. The last section is poetical in form, with a quotation from the Old Testament.


## Second year, morning

*I Samuel 24.9–17*
This is part of the story of how David spares the life of Saul, the king, at a time when David is outlawed and Saul is seeking to capture him. David's refusal to injure Saul is out of respect for the anointed king and fear of God's judgment. The consequence of this incident is that Saul gives David his blessing and assures him that he will succeed to the throne.


*Galatians 6.1–10*
Near the end of his letter, Paul gives practical illustrations of the love that Christians are to show. They are to give help to fellow Christians who have sinned; they are to share their wealth with those who teach them; they are to do good to all men.


*Luke 7.36–50*
Luke tells a story which contrasts Jesus's attitude to an outcast of society with that of a Pharisee. This is followed by a parable which illustrates how love springs from forgiveness.


## Second year, evening

*I Samuel 18.1–16*
The writer describes how David becomes a member of king Saul's court and a commander in the army. The passage also contrasts David's friendship for Jonathan with the suspicion and envy shown by Saul.


*Matthew 7.13–27*
Towards the end of the Sermon on the Mount, Matthew includes a collection of sayings about doing the will of the Father and producing fruit in the Christian life.

*Tenth Sunday after Pentecost*

## ASB
## Year 1

*Job 42.1–6*   Preface as above.

*Philippians 2.1–11*
Paul invites the Christians at Philippi to cultivate within their fellowship a quality of life based on communion with Christ. He recalls the example of Christ, particularly his humility and self-denial for the sake of others. Part of this passage is thought to be an early Christian hymn on the theme of the humiliation and exaltation of Christ.

*John 13.1–15*   See Maundy Thursday. First year.

## Year 2

Prefaces as above.

# Eleventh Sunday after Pentecost
(Trinity 10)

## The Serving Community

### First year, morning

*Isaiah 42.1–7*    See First Sunday after Epiphany. Second year,
morning.

*II Corinthians 4.1–10*
The ministry of Paul has been attacked and rejected by some of the
Christians at Corinth. Paul believes that only those who are in
darkness can fail to see the light of the gospel he preaches, for that
gospel is Christ himself. In defence of his apostleship, Paul gives a
graphic description of his ministry, claiming that in his adversities,
as in the suffering and death of Jesus, the power of God is at work.

*John 13.33–36*
The writer of John's Gospel records the command that the disciples
are to love one another. This command is set in the context of Jesus's
departure and indicates how the disciples are to govern their
community life after his death; it is referred to as a 'new' commandment because it belongs to the 'new age' introduced by Jesus.

### First year, evening

*Exodus 18.13–26*
The writer tells how Jethro advises Moses to appoint judges over
the people to share with him the administration of justice. Moses is
to decide only the more important matters and give general direction
about the application of the law. In this way, the law retains its
divine authority, and Moses is still the people's representative
before God.

*Acts 6.1–15*
The writer tells of the appointment of seven men to assist the
apostles in their work among Christians at Jerusalem. One of these
men, Stephen, is portrayed as a man of particular power and
wisdom. He was probably the leader of a group of Greek-speaking
Jews, referred to here as the Hellenists.

*Eleventh Sunday after Pentecost*

## Second year, morning

*I Chronicles 29.1–9*
This passage is part of David's final address to his officers about his plans for the temple, to be built after his death by Solomon. He challenges the assembly to give generously to this project by promising gifts of gold and silver and other materials from his own treasures. The response is a generous one.

*Philippians 1.1–11*
Paul opens his letter to the Christians at Philippi with his customary greeting, followed by an expression of thanks for the support that they have given him during his imprisonment. The Philippians had sent Paul a gift, and he sees this as evidence of their partnership with him in the gospel.

*Luke 17.5–10*
Jesus is here teaching about faith and service. In the passage on faith, it is possible that the sycamine tree is an indirect reference to Judaism. The passage on service makes plain that Christian disciples are to serve God without any thought of reward.

## Second year, evening

*II Chronicles 24.8–14*
The temple has been pillaged by worshippers of the Baals, the fertility gods of the Canaanites, and the Chronicler now tells how money is collected for its restoration.

*Matthew 21.28–32*
Matthew tells the parable of the two sons, in which the repentant son is commended for his eventual obedience. The parable signifies God's judgment on Israel for her disobedience and his welcome of repentant sinners.

## ASB
**Year 1**

*Isaiah 42.1–7* See First Sunday after Epiphany. Second year, morning.

*II Corinthians 4.1–10*   Preface as above.

*John 13.31–35*   Preface as above for John 13.33–36.

## Year 2

*I Chronicles 29.1–9*   Preface as above.

*Philippians 1.1–11*   Preface as above.

*Matthew 20.1–16*   See Fifth Sunday after Epiphany. Second year, morning.

# Twelfth Sunday after Pentecost
(Trinity 11)

---

## *The Witnessing Community*

### First year, morning

*Isaiah 49.1–6*   See Epiphany. First year.

*II Corinthians 5.14–6.2*
Paul defends his ministry by claiming that it is controlled by the love of Christ. It is from Christ that he has received his ministry of reconciliation; he therefore urges the Corinthians to be reconciled to God and to accept his own ministry among them. The reference to Christ being made 'to be sin' indicates the extent of his identification with us.

*John 17.20–26*
This passage is written as part of a prayer offered by Jesus shortly before his death. He has prayed for himself and his disciples; now he prays for later generations of believers, asking especially that their unity may reflect that of the Son with the Father. The prayer indicates the writer's concern for unity and mission within his own Christian community.

### First year, evening

*Ezekiel 33.1–9, 30–33*
In the first part of this passage, the prophet Ezekiel describes himself as a watchman, whose responsibility is to protect the people by warning them of approaching danger. In the second part, he describes himself as a minstrel to whom the people listen but whose words they do not obey. Both images illustrate the prophet's role as a witness to whose message the people should respond.

*Acts 16.6–15*
The writer describes how Paul and his companions, perhaps including the writer, are directed by the Spirit to Macedonia. Here they meet a woman called Lydia, whose house later becomes the centre for Christian work in Philippi. This passage illustrates the writer's

conviction that the spread of the gospel is under the direct guidance
of the Spirit of God.

## Second year, morning

*Micah 4.1–7*
In words very similar to a passage in Isaiah, the prophet Micah
records a vision of a new Jerusalem which will be the religious centre
of the world. This hope is more fully developed by later prophets
during the exile of the Jews in Babylon.

*Acts 17.22–31*
This passage contains the account of Paul's speech in Athens, in
which he identifies the unknown God of the Athenians with the true
God who raised Jesus from the dead. The writer is therefore
asserting that Christianity is the fulfilment of Greek religion. The
incident takes place at the Areopagus, a public debating place where
philosophers gathered to exchange ideas.

*Matthew 5.13–16*
In this passage from the Sermon on the Mount, the images of salt
and light are used to suggest the nature of true discipleship. In
Jewish thought, salt is associated with wisdom, and this passage may
imply that Christian disciples, not the representatives of Jewish
wisdom, are the truly wise who now show God's light to the world.

## Second year, evening

*Ruth 2.1–17*
Ruth, the Moabitess, now a widow, has travelled to Bethlehem with
her mother-in-law, Naomi. Here, she meets Boaz, one of Naomi's
relations, whom she later marries, thus becoming an ancestor of
David. The writer has used this beautiful and ancient story to suggest
that the Jews should welcome relationships with other peoples.

*III John*
This brief letter reflects the struggle for leadership in an early
Christian community. The writer commends Gaius, to whom this
letter is addressed, for his sound doctrine and behaviour, and
criticizes Diotrephes for his ambition and rejection of the writer's
authority.

**ASB**
**Year 1**

*Isaiah 49.1–6* See Epiphany. First year. Preface for Isaiah 49.1–13.

Other Prefaces as above.

# Thirteenth Sunday after Pentecost
(Trinity 12)

*The Suffering Community*

**First year, morning**

*Isaiah 50.4–9*
The prophet expresses in personal terms the thoughts of the people in exile. They recognize that they deserve punishment and are bearing their humiliation with courage. Their trust is still in God, for they believe he will soon come to save them.

*I Peter 4.12–19*
The writer addresses a community facing persecution and tries to sustain them in their suffering. Such persecution serves as a test of faith; but it is also a sharing in Christ's sufferings and is therefore a reason for rejoicing. The quotation near the end of the passage is from the book of Proverbs.

*John 16.1–11*
In this passage, the writer records how Jesus warns Christians about the persecution they may expect when he leaves them. But they are also promised that the Spirit will come to strengthen them. He will also judge the world for its failure to believe in Jesus.

**First year, evening**

*II Kings 19.8–19*
The writer has described the siege of Jerusalem by Sennacherib, king of Assyria. Now he records the prayer for help that king Hezekiah offers to God when he receives a threatening letter from Sennacherib demanding surrender. Following this passage, the story tells of Isaiah's support for Hezekiah in his resistance when under siege, and of the outbreak of plague in the Assyrian camp which forces Sennacherib to withdraw.

*Acts 16.16–40*
The writer tells the story of the arrest and imprisonment of Paul and Silas at Philippi as a result of their healing of a fortune-teller. Their

gaoler is converted. Paul then protests to the authorities at the treatment they have received, since it was illegal to beat a Roman citizen. The story is an illustration of the belief that deliverance is brought about by the intervention of God.


## Second year, morning

*Jeremiah 12.1–6*
These verses belong to the confessions of Jeremiah, a collection of very personal passages, scattered throughout the book, which reveal the innermost thoughts of the prophet, especially his weariness with the task God has given him. Here, Jeremiah asks searching questions about the meaning of life and the state of his own country.

*Acts 20.17–35*
This is Paul's farewell speech to the leaders of the church at Ephesus who have come to Miletus to meet him on his way to Jerusalem. Though defensive in tone, the speech gives encouragement to the elders to maintain the life of the church.

*Matthew 10.16–22*
Matthew records the instructions given by Jesus to his disciples before he sends them out on mission. This part of the address is chiefly concerned with likely responses to the disciples and how they should react to them. In their present form, the instructions probably reflect the experience of missionaries sent out from the writer's own church.


## Second year, evening

*Exodus 5.1–6.1*
This is part of the story of Moses' attempt to persuade the Pharaoh to let the Israelites go free. He asks permission for them to go into the wilderness for a feast, but the only result is that they have to make bricks without straw. They complain. Moses then prays to God and is reassured by his promise of help.

*Hebrews 12.1–14*
After listing in the previous chapter examples of faith from the history of Israel, the writer now calls on his readers to endure

hostility with the courage shown by their ancestors and by Jesus himself. He explains their present suffering as part of the discipline that will lead them to holiness. The passage includes a quotation from the book of Proverbs.

**ASB**
**Year 1**

*Isaiah 50.4–9a*   Preface as above.

*Acts 7.54–8.1*
Following his speech to the Sanhedrin, Stephen has a vision of Jesus, the glorified Son of man. To the Jews this is the ultimate blasphemy and Stephen is stoned to death. There are resemblances in the story to the death of Jesus himself.

*John 16.1–11*   Preface as above.

**Year 2**

*Jeremiah 20.7–11a*   See Fourth Sunday after Pentecost. First year, evening. Preface for Jeremiah 20.7–13.

*Acts 20.17–35*   Preface as above.

*Matthew 10.16–22*   Preface as above.

# Fourteenth Sunday after Pentecost
(Trinity 13)

## The Neighbour

**First year, morning**

*Leviticus 19.9–18*
These laws are part of the Holiness Code, in which Israel i commanded to be holy because God is holy. They insist upon hones and compassionate behaviour.

*Romans 12.9–21*
Paul is here setting out instructions for Christian behaviour. It i possible that this, with other similar passages in the New Testamen formed a code of conduct generally accepted in the early church.

*Luke 10.25–37*
In answer to a lawyer's question about the identity of his neighbou Jesus tells the parable of the Good Samaritan, in which human nee is shown to be of more concern than ritual laws or racial prejudice The priest and the Levite will not risk ritual uncleanness by touchin what might be a dead body, but the Samaritan does not allow raci prejudice to impede his compassion.

**First year, evening**

*Proverbs 25.6–22*
This collection of proverbs, written down during the reign Hezekiah, is largely made up of couplets which illustrate the gener theme of good behaviour towards one's neighbour. Proverbs is book of religious education meant to encourage the development sound character.

*Luke 14.7–14*
Luke records a parable, told by Jesus at a dinner in a Pharisee house, which criticizes the proud and commends the humble. Th second part of the passage emphasizes the writer's concern for th helpless and the needy.

## Second year, morning

### Deuteronomy 15.7–11

This passage is concerned with the care of the poor in the community, and particularly whether they should be lent money, in the light of the ancient practice of cancelling debts every seven years. The law applies only to fellow Israelites.

### John 4.15–21

Throughout this letter, the writer urges members of his Christian community to treat one another as God has treated them, in love. He suggests that loving one another is proof of their love for God.

### Luke 16.19–31

The parable of Lazarus and the rich man is possibly based upon a popular folk story. It illustrates the concern for the poor shown in this Gospel and, by implication, criticizes the leaders of Judaism for their attitude towards outcasts and Gentiles.

## Second year, evening

### Deuteronomy 16.13–20

The writer is describing the feasts to be observed in Israel: he has written about the feast of the Passover and the feast of Weeks, both in the springtime; now he describes the autumn feast of Tabernacles, or Booths, which probably began as a festival at the time of the wine harvest. The booths were shelters erected in the fields and they became associated with the tents, or booths used at the time of the exodus from Egypt. The passage concludes with an instruction about the appointment of judges.

### James 3.13–4.12

The writer of this letter describes the life of the truly wise man: it is peaceful, and without selfishness or pretence. He goes on to speak of the need for peace within the community, and commends to all the virtue of humility.

*Fourteenth Sunday after Pentecost*

## ASB
**Year 1**

*Proverbs 31.10 – end*
This passage describes the life and character of a good wife; she i
the industrious household manager; she provides for the needs o
her husband and family. Such a life of service deserves the highes
praise.

*Ephesians 5.25–6.4*
The writer has dealt with various aspects of Christian conduct an
now gives instructions about domestic life. The relationship betwee
husband and wife is used to describe the relationship between Chris
and the church.

*Mark 10.2–16*   See Fifteenth Sunday after Pentecost. First year
morning.

**Year 2**

*Genesis 45.1–15*   See Fifteenth Sunday after Pentecost. Secon
year, morning.

*Ephesians 3.14 – end*
The writer has reminded his readers that he has been called to be a
apostle to the Gentiles as part of God's plan that the whole worl
should be saved. Now he prays for them, that they should hav
fellowship with Christ and know his love.

*Luke 11.1–13*   See Sixteenth Sunday after Pentecost. Second year
morning.

# Fifteenth Sunday after Pentecost
(Trinity 14)

*The Family*

**First year, morning**

*Isaiah 54.1–8*
In this passage, Israel is assured that although she has suffered humiliation in exile, God still cares for her. She has been like a barren woman or a woman separated from her husband, but she will come to rejoice as if she were God's wife and the bearer of many children.

*Ephesians 5.21–6.4*
The writer has dealt with various aspects of Christian conduct and now gives instructions about domestic life. He writes according to the understanding of his time. The relationship between husband and wife is used to describe the relationship between Christ and the church.

*Mark 10.2–16*
Mark has placed together two incidents relating to family life. In the first, Jesus responds to a question about divorce with a statement of the ideal of marriage. His further comment about divorce, stricter than the corresponding statement in Matthew, treats men and women equally, whereas Jewish law allowed divorce only to men. In the second incident, Jesus shows his love for children.

**First year, evening**

*Genesis 29.9–20*
The writer tells the story of how Jacob meets Rachel, falls in love with her and agrees to serve her father Laban for seven years in return for her hand in marriage. The incident is part of a long narrative containing traditions about the origin of the twelve tribes of Israel.

*Mark 3.31–35*
Mark records how the family of Jesus come seeking him. Jesus responds to the news of their arrival by saying that obedience to

*Fifteenth Sunday after Pentecost*

God is more important than family ties. This was a message of particular relevance to a persecuted Christian community such as that addressed in this Gospel.

## Second year, morning

*Genesis 45.1–15*
This passage is from the cycle of stories about Joseph containing traditions of the early history of Israel. Joseph has been supplying grain to his brothers, who have not recognized him. What follows is a moving story of Joseph's love for his family and his willingness to forgive his brothers.

*I Peter 3.1–9*
The writer addresses different groups within the church: he has spoken to slaves; now he turns to wives and husbands. The wives are possibly those married to non-Christian husbands. The author, who writes out of the understanding of his time, sees family life as the context for Christian obedience.

*Luke 14.25–33*
Luke records Jesus's words to the crowds who were following him to Jerusalem, words which express vividly the sacrifice involved in discipleship. Disciples must be prepared to break all family ties if they are to share his life, and they are urged to count the cost before committing themselves.

## Second year, evening

*Genesis 47.1–12*
After Joseph had made himself known to his brothers when they came to Egypt to buy corn, he sent for his father to join them. This passage completes the story of how the family came to settle in Egypt. They are welcomed by the Pharaoh and given the best land.

*Luke 10.38–42*
This is the story of Jesus's visit to the house of Martha and Mary. The attitude shown by Mary is commended as the ideal of Christian discipleship.

# ASB
## Year 1

See Sixteenth Sunday after Pentecost. First year, morning.

## Year 2

*I Kings 3.4–15*　See Sixteenth Sunday after Pentecost. Second year, morning.

*I Timothy 2.1–7*　See Sixteenth Sunday after Pentecost. Second year, morning.

*Matthew 14.1–12*
This is the account of the death of John the Baptist, killed by Herod Antipas, the son of Herod the Great, who had inherited Galilee from his father. It illustrates the danger of fame to Jesus and explains why he began to withdraw from too public a ministry.

# Sixteenth Sunday after Pentecost
(Trinity 15)

---

## Those in Authority

### First year, morning

*Isaiah 45.1–7*
The prophet hails Cyrus, king of Persia and conqueror of the
Babylonian empire, as God's anointed, because he hopes that Cyrus
will let the Jewish exiles return home. The use of the term 'anointed'
means that Cyrus is acting under God's authority. It is therefore
God himself who brings about the release of his people.

*Romans 13.1–7*
Paul urges the Roman Christians to obey the lawful authorities of
the Empire, not least by paying their taxes. He believes that the
power of the authorities is derived from God: to resist the state
would therefore be to resist God. At the time when Paul wrote, the
state was maintaining the order and justice which permitted him to
travel and preach freely.

*Matthew 22.15–22*
Matthew describes how Jesus avoids the trap set by the Pharisees
and the supporters of Herod, who hope to trick him into making a
politically compromising statement. Jesus brushes aside the political
issue of the recognition of Rome's power and raises the more
fundamental question of duty to God.

### First year, evening

*Daniel 5.17–30*
Daniel interprets writing which has appeared on the wall during
King Belshazzar's feast, a feast at which the gold and silver vessels
taken from the temple at Jerusalem are being used. The writing
warns that Belshazzar will be punished not only for this act of
sacrilege, but also for his arrogant attitude towards God. This
incident marks the end of the Babylonian empire and the beginning
of the rule of the Persians, under which the Jewish exiles were
allowed to return home.

*Luke 12.13–21*
In response to a listener's request for help, Luke tells the parable of the rich fool. The story warns against covetousness and preoccupation with worldly possessions.

## Second year, morning

*I Kings 3.5–15*
King Solomon has a dream, in which God offers him a choice of gift. Solomon's request for understanding and wise judgment reflects the Jewish tradition about the wisdom of his rule; the additional gift of earthly riches refers to the splendour of his reign. This passage shows how dreams were thought to be a means of divine communication.

*I Timothy 2.1–7*
The writer urges Christians to pray for all men. These prayers include intercessions for the Roman authorities, probably in the hope that such loyalty will lead to a more peaceful life for Christians. The concern for all men arises out of the writer's belief in one God who has made himself known in Jesus Christ.

*Luke 11.1–13*
Jesus teaches his disciples to pray. First, they are taught the Lord's prayer; second, they are told a parable illustrating God's willingness to respond to their requests. For the writer of this Gospel, the greatest gift to be received from God in answer to prayer is the gift of the Holy Spirit.

## Second year, evening

*I Kings 12.1–16*
This is the story of how Rehoboam inherits Solomon's kingdom but causes the northern tribes to revolt by threatening them with heavier demands than his father. As a result of the rebellion, Rehoboam is left with only the two southern tribes of Judah while Jeroboam becomes king of the ten northern tribes, now called Israel.

*Luke 16.1–13*
Luke records a difficult parable: the story of the dishonest steward, who gains friends through accepting less payment for debts than is

due. Maybe the servant is commended for acting promptly in a crisis, or for his shrewdness or for fulfilling the spirit of the Jewish law by forgoing interest on the debts. Luke then urges people to use their own money to make friends, which pleases God. The reason why money is called 'the unrighteous mammon' is that it is the great rival of God for human devotion and service.


## ASB
**Year 1**

See Fourteenth Sunday after Pentecost. First year, morning.

**Year 2**

See Fourteenth Sunday after Pentecost. Second year, morning.

# Seventeenth Sunday after Pentecost
(Trinity 16)

## The Proof of Faith

### First year, morning

*Jeremiah 7.1–7*
Jeremiah addresses the people coming to the harvest festival in the autumn of 608 BC, a time of political uncertainty. The prophet attacks the belief that Jerusalem can never be captured, a belief based on Isaiah's prophecy a century earlier that the temple would not fall. Jeremiah calls for faith in the temple to be replaced by a spirit of repentance and a return to righteousness.

*James 1.22–27*
James calls for a practical religion which bears witness to what is believed. For him, the proof of religion lies in the help given to those who are in need. By 'the world' in the last verse, he means society in its opposition to God.

*Matthew 7.21–29*
In this closing section of the sermon on the mount, Matthew stresses that a disciple must not merely profess faith, but obey God's will. For the writer, doing the will of God means following the teaching of Jesus as found in this sermon.

### First year, evening

*Joshua 6.1–20*
This is the story of the capture of the city of Jericho by Joshua during the period of the settlement of the promised land. Following the collapse of the walls, the whole city is destroyed as a sacrifice to God and the captured treasure is set aside for sacred use.

*John 6.53–69*
Following the feeding of the five thousand, Jesus is described as the bread of life and this passage records the offence that this description causes. The teaching here seems to reflect the early church's

understanding of the Lord's Supper: sharing in the body of Christ in faith brings eternal life.

## Second year, morning

*Jeremiah 32.6–15*
Jeremiah describes how God has told him to buy his cousin's field, at a time when the land has already been captured by the Babylonians and the people are being taken into exile. His purchase of the land is an acted parable, expressing his faith in the future of his country.

*Galatians 2.20–3.9*
Paul quotes his own experience of the living Christ and the Galatians' experience of the Spirit to show that men are justified by God rather than through their obedience to the law. The example of Abraham shows that the proper response to God is one of faith.

*Luke 7.1–10*
Luke illustrates the faith of a Gentile believer through the story of the healing of the centurion's slave. Jesus does not actually meet the centurion: his faith in Jesus makes this unnecessary. Furthermore, the centurion knows that, according to Jewish law, Jesus should not enter a Gentile house. For the writer, this incident anticipates the mission of the church to the Gentiles.

## Second year, evening

*Judges 7.1–8, 19–23*
This story tells how Gideon, a local tribal leader, captures the camp of the Midianites with a very small army. According to the writer, Gideon's forces are deliberately made smaller to illustrate God's power at work in those who trust in him.

*John 7.1–17*
The writer of John's Gospel records the visit of Jesus to Jerusalem at the time of the feast of Tabernacles. Despite pressure from his brothers, Jesus is unwilling to go to Jerusalem until he is sure that the time is right and that it is God's will. At Jerusalem, Jesus shows that he wants his teaching accepted because it is from God.

ASB
**Year 1**

*Jeremiah 7.1–11*   Preface as above for Jeremiah 7.1–7.

*James 1.16–end*   Preface as above.

*Luke 17.11–19*   See Fifth Sunday after Pentecost. Second year, morning.

**Year 2**

*Jeremiah 32.6–15*   Preface as above.

*Galatians 2.15–3.9*
Paul asserts that men are justified by faith in Christ and not by obedience to the law. In confirmation of his argument he appeals to his own experience of the living Christ and the Galatians' experience of the Spirit. The example of Abraham shows that the proper response to God is one of faith.

*Luke 7.1–10*   Preface as above.

# Eighteenth Sunday after Pentecost
(Trinity 17)

*The Offering of Life*

### First year, morning

*Deuteronomy 26.1–11*
This chapter records an ancient law that the first-fruits of the harvest should be presented to God in gratitude for his blessings. The offering therefore is accompanied by a recital of the basic Israelite creed, acknowledging what God has done for his people. The writer, reflecting the practice of his own day after the building of the temple, says that the offering should be made at the central shrine in Jerusalem.

*II Corinthians 8.1–9*
Paul tells the Corinthian church of the generosity that Christians in Macedonia have shown in response to his request for money for the poor at Jerusalem. He urges the Corinthians to respond in the same way. Paul relates their giving to what God has done for them, in Jesus.

*Matthew 5.21–26*
This is the first of six examples given in the Sermon on the Mount of the way in which the Christian life fulfils and exceeds the commands of the Jewish law. Christians are urged not to be angry with one another and not to divorce their worship from their relationship with fellow Christians. The punishments mentioned are not so much to be taken literally as to indicate the seriousness of the offences.

### First year, evening

*Exodus 32.1–6, 15–20*
This story of the making of a golden calf while Moses is on the mountain demonstrates the people's desire to have a god they can see. When Moses returns and discovers what has happened, he not only destroys the idol they have made but also breaks the stones on which the law is inscribed. His action symbolizes the people's lack of fitness to receive God's law.

*John 12.1–8*
The writer of John's Gospel tells how Mary anoints the feet of Jesus.
Perhaps the writer understood this act of anointing as a declaration
of the kingship of Jesus, for it is as king that Jesus is shortly to enter
Jerusalem.

## Second year, morning

*Nehemiah 6.1–16*
The Chronicler records the various attempts by the Samaritan
leaders to prevent the Jews who have returned from exile from
rebuilding the walls of Jerusalem. Nehemiah is not deceived by their
schemes and presses on to complete the walls. The writer sees this
achievement as a reversal of fortune, both for the Samaritans, who
have previously exercised authority over Jerusalem, and for the
Jews, who now have a secure home.

*I Peter 4.7–11*
In view of the early Christian belief in the nearness of the end of the
world, with its inevitable judgment, the writer urges his readers to
show love to one another.

*Matthew 25.14–29*
The parable of the talents is here seen as a guide to the way Christians
should act during the absence of Christ. They are assured of reward
at the time of his return, according to what they have achieved
during his absence. The writer uses the early belief in the imminent
return of Christ to encourage right and wise conduct.

## Second year, evening

*I Chronicles 29.10–20*
This is part of the Chronicler's account of David's final address to
Israel. This section of the speech is a prayer, probably reflecting the
prayers used in the writer's own day. It expresses David's thankful-
ness to God and records the provision he has made for the building
of the temple by Solomon, his successor.

*II Corinthians 9.1–15*
Paul reminds his Corinthian readers of the collection he is making
for the poor at Jerusalem and urges them to have their gift ready in

*Eighteenth Sunday after Pentecost*

time. As an encouragement to the Corinthians to respond to hi
request, he describes the merits of generosity and thanksgiving. The
passage includes a quotation from Psalm 112.


## ASB
### Year 1

*Deuteronomy 26.1–11*   Preface as above.

*II Corinthians 8.1–9*   Preface as above.

*Matthew 5.17–26*
After asserting the value of the law, Matthew records the first of six
examples in the Sermon on the Mount of the way in which the
Christian life fulfils and exceeds its commands. Christians are urged
not to be angry with one another and not to divorce their worship
from their relationship with fellow Christians. The punishments
mentioned are not so much to be taken literally as to indicate the
seriousness of the offences.

### Year 2

*Nehemiah 6.1–16*   Preface as above.

*Ecclesiasticus 38.24 – end*
The writer contrasts the life of the scholar with that of the craftsman.
Each is a wise man in his own way: the skill of the craftsman sustains
the life of the city; without scholars there would be no politics and
no legal system. But the craftsman is judged to be closer to reality
and to God.

*I Peter 4.7–11*   Preface as above.

*Matthew 25.14–30*   Preface as above.

# Nineteenth Sunday after Pentecost
(Trinity 18)

*The Life of Faith*

**First year, morning**

*Genesis 28.10–22*
This is the story of Jacob's dream at Bethel, presented here as his
first encounter with the God of his forefathers. It is a story of Jacob's
discovery of a God who is awesome, yet interested in him and his
descendants. Jacob responds with fear; but he also seeks to make a
bargain: if the Lord will look after him, then the Lord will be his
God.

*Hebrews 11.1–3, 7–16*
The writer introduces his recital of the faith of the elders of Israel
with a statement of his own understanding of faith. He then
illustrates this understanding by referring to the lives of Noah,
Abraham and Sarah, all of whom lived, like pilgrims, in faith.

*Luke 5.1–11*
Luke records the miraculous catch of fish and the call of Peter,
James and John. The miracle is a parable of the spread of the gospel;
the call of Peter shows that he is the one chosen to lead the mission
of the church to the wider world.

**First year, evening**

*Job 23.1–10*
Job responds to the charge of Eliphaz that his questioning has led
him into unbelief by claiming that he is still earnestly seeking God.
He believes that a confrontation with God will vindicate him.

*John 5.1–16*
The writer of John's Gospel records the reaction of the Jewish
authorities to the healing of a paralysed man on the Sabbath.
Throughout the incident, Jesus takes the initiative, both in the
healing of the man and later in identifying himself. It is a feature of

this Gospel's presentation of Jesus that he is always in control of events.


## Second year, morning

*Daniel 6.10–23*
This is the story of how Daniel defies the order that prayer should be offered only to Darius the king. The order had been proposed by the enemies of Daniel at court who were jealous of his position and influence. Daniel remains faithful to God who, according to the story, enables him to escape from the lions. 'Daniel in the lions' den' was remembered and retold as an encouragement to Jews in later generations to hold fast to their faith.


*Romans 5.1–11*
Paul outlines some of the consequences of belief in Christ: peace with God, access to his grace and the gift of his love. The 'wrath of God' indicates, in Paul's view, God's personal reaction to sin, but the death of Christ reconciles sinners to God.


*Luke 19.1–10*
Luke recounts how Zacchaeus the tax collector, an outcast in Jewish society because of his occupation, is treated by Jesus as a true son of Abraham. The story is used to illustrate the ministry of Jesus to those rejected by society.


## Second year, evening

*Deuteronomy 30.11–20*   See Sixth Sunday before Easter. First year, morning.


*II Thessalonians 2.13–3.5*
Paul has described the fate of those who oppose Christ. Now, in contrast, he gives thanks for the lives of the Thessalonian Christians and urges them to be firm in their faith. In conclusion, Paul invites the Thessalonians to pray for him, and expresses his confidence in them.

**ASB**
**Year 1**

*Genesis 28.10 – end*   Preface as above.

*Hebrews 11.1–2, 8–16*
The writer begins with a definition of faith. He then illustrates this understanding by referring to the lives of Abraham and Sarah who lived, like pilgrims, in faith.

*Matthew 6.24 – end*   See Fifth Sunday before Christmas. Second year, evening

**Year 2**

Prefaces as above.

# Twentieth Sunday after Pentecost
(Trinity 19)

*Citizens of Heaven*

**First year, morning**

*Jeremiah 29.1, 4–14*
In the first part of his letter to the exiles, Jeremiah urges the people to settle down to their new life and not to be led astray by false prophets who might think up some hasty scheme for a return home. At the same time, he promises an eventual end to the exile and the restoration of the people to their own land. In the meantime, the prophet assures his people that God can be experienced and worshipped in Babylon.

*Philippians 3.7–21*
Paul has listed his advantages as a Jew; now he describes them as a hindrance to fellowship with Christ and is glad to renounce them. He presses on to the goal of perfection and urges the Philippian Christians to follow his example, so that they may all be members of Christ's kingdom when he comes to reign.

*John 17.1–10*
This passage is presented as the opening part of a prayer offered by Jesus shortly before his death. It emphasizes that Jesus has been obedient to the Father and has revealed him to his disciples. In this part of the prayer, Jesus is concerned mainly for his disciples, because it is through them that the world will hear the gospel message.

**First year, evening**

*Ezekiel 11.14–20*
The prophet records God's words of consolation and hope to those in exile in Babylon. The consolation is that, even though they are in a foreign land, God has not forsaken them but can be found just where they are. The hope is contained in the promise that God will return them to their own land.

186

*II Timothy 4.6–18*
This passage speaks of the writer's trial and his approaching death. God has strengthened him in his suffering and, though he will soon die, God will keep him safe until the kingdom comes.

## Second year, morning

*Isaiah 33.17–22*
The prophet has spoken of disaster facing the nation: perhaps some threat to the city of Jerusalem. Now he describes a happy future, when the splendour of God as king will be seen and the nation will be secure from her enemies. The passage is a poem or a song, greeting the coming of God's rule.

*Revelation 7.9–17*
The prophet records in poetic language his vision of the worship of God by peoples from every nation. Those who have suffered for their faith have eternal life in the presence of God. The passage is meant to encourage the prophet's contemporaries before they experience the final strugle with evil which the writer expects.

*Matthew 25.1–13*
Matthew records the parable of the wise and foolish bridesmaids, using the image of a wedding feast to represent the coming kingdom of God. Christians are warned to keep alert and to be prepared for the expected day of judgment.

## Second year, evening

*Micah 7.7–10a, 18–20*
In a situation of almost universal mistrust, the prophet expresses his own trust in God, and affirms his belief that God will forgive and restore his people. The prophet therefore offers his praises to God.

*Revelation 21.10–14, 22.1–5*
These two passages are part of the writer's imaginative vision of a new heaven and a new earth. In the first passage, he sees the new Jerusalem, built on the foundation of the apostles. In the second, he sees a river and a tree, symbols of life, in the heavenly city where God will reign for ever. This vision recalls the garden of Eden with its river and its tree of life.

## Twentieth Sunday after Pentecost

## ASB
## Year 1

*Daniel 3.13–26*  See Twenty-first Sunday after Pentecost. First year, morning.

*Romans 8.18–25*
In a passage full of hope, Paul looks to the future of creation and mankind. Although there is present suffering, Christians are awaiting their new birth as the adopted sons of God. They must do so in hope and patience.

*Luke 9.51 – end*  See Twenty-first Sunday after Pentecost. First year, morning.

## Year 2

*Genesis 32.22–30*
In preparation for meeting his brother, Esau, Jacob has dispatched presents to appease him. He now sends his own family away for safety. He spends the night in an encounter with God, referred to in this story as wrestling with a man. The significance of knowing names is to be found in the ancient belief that to know the name of a man or a god is to have access to his power. This story marks the climax of Jacob's relationship with God and describes his being given a new name as the ancestor of the tribes of Israel.

*I Corinthians 9.19 – end*   See Twenty-first Sunday after Pentecost. Second year, morning.

*Matthew 7.13–27*
In a passage which seems to be directed to disciples in the early church, Matthew records a collection of sayings of Jesus about producing fruit in the Christian life and doing the will of the Father. The opening verses emphasized the difficulty of the Christian way. The closing verses stress the need to obey the words of Jesus.

# Twenty-first Sunday after Pentecost
(Trinity 20)

## *Endurance*

### First year, morning

*Daniel 3.13–25*
This is part of the story of the rescue of three men from the furnace into which they had been thrown for their refusal to worship the golden image erected by king Nebuchadnezzar. The story, set in the time of the exile in Babylon, is told to encourage later Jews to hold fast to their faith when they too are tempted to worship idols set up by a foreign ruler.

*Hebrews 11.32–12.2*
The writer concludes his list of men of faith with an account of their tribulations. He then appeals to his readers that, in the presence of such witnesses, they should persevere in faith, following the example of Jesus.

*Luke 9.51–62*
Luke begins his long account of the journey of Jesus to Jerusalem, which will end in his death and glory. The refusal of the Samaritan village to receive him is a foretaste of what is to come in Jerusalem. The replies of Jesus to those who are thinking of following him indicate the total commitment required of a disciple.

### First year, evening

*Isaiah 32.1–8*
The prophet describes what would happen if there were a righteous king on the throne: he would protect the people and end injustice. In its tone of moral instruction, this passage resembles teaching found in the book of Proverbs.

*Hebrews 10.23–39*
The writer urges his fellow Christians to remain true to the Christian faith and not to fall away. He warns them against such apostasy by stressing the severity of the judgment they would receive. The

warning is followed by an exhortation to have faith and a plea for endurance in time of trial. The passage includes a number of quotations from the Old Testament.

## Second year, morning

*Genesis 32.24–30*
In preparation for meeting his brother, Esau, Jacob has dispatched presents to appease him and sent his own family away for safety. He now spends the night in an encounter with God, referred to in this story as wrestling with a man. The significance of knowing names is to be found in the ancient belief that to know the name of a man or a god is to have access to his power. This story marks the climax of Jacob's relationship with God and describes his being given a new name as the ancestor of the tribes of Israel.

*I Corinthians 9.19–27*
Paul describes the lengths to which he goes in order to commend Christ to his fellows. Then, using the illustration of a race, he says that the crown to be won in the Christian life is a more lasting prize than the olive wreath awarded at the games.

*Matthew 7.13–20*
In a passage which seems to be directed to disciples in the early church, Matthew records teaching about the need to produce fruit in the Christian life. The opening verses emphasize the difficulty of the Christian way.

## Second year, evening

*Ecclesiastes 12.1–14*
The preacher recognizes that youth is a time for making the most of life, but urges the young not to forget God. In contrast to the abandon of youth, the preacher, something of a pessimist, paints a picture of the problems of old age, followed only by death. In an appendix, the book closes with a word of praise for the teaching of the preacher.

*II Peter 1.1–11*
The letter opens with the customary greeting and then reminds the readers of Christ's power, given to Christians to enable them to live

a good life. The rest of the passage is an encouragement to virtue and a promise of reward for those who are faithful.


# ASB
# Year 1

*Habakkuk 2.1–4*
The prophet climbs a watch tower to seek a revelation from God which he then writes on a tablet to preserve for the future. The message is clear: only those who remain loyal to God will survive; the wicked will be judged. In the writer's mind this is the answer to the question of why God allows the wicked to oppress the righteous, but the answer has been taken by New Testament writers to refer to victory for those who believe in Jesus.

*Acts 26.1–8*
After his arrest and appeal to Caesar, Paul is handed over by Festus to Agrippa. These verses are the opening of Paul's defence before Agrippa and show that he is concerned only to defend his relationship to Judaism: he has lived as a Pharisee who rests his hope on God. Why should those who believe in a general resurrection object to his claim that Jesus has been raised from the dead?

*Luke 18.1–8*
Luke uses the parable of the unjust judge to suggest that the kingdom of God will come in response to the persistent prayers of Christian people. In the meantime, Christians are urged to remain faithful as they await the coming of Christ.

# Year 2

*Ezekiel 12.21 – end*
This passage contains two prophetic oracles. Both reflect the popular response to Ezekiel's message of judgement: people do not believe that he has anything to say to their generation. So both oracles affirm that the prophet's vision is not false and that God will quickly act to vindicate him.

*I Peter 1.13–21*   See Fourth Sunday after Easter. First year, evening. Preface for I Peter 1.10–21.

*Twenty-first Sunday after Pentecost*

*John 11.17–27*  See Third Sunday after Easter. Second year, morning.

# Twenty-second Sunday after Pentecost
(Trinity 21)

The theme and readings for this Sunday are the same as for the Sixth Sunday after Epiphany, though the themes and readings for the First year and the Second year are in reverse order.

ASB
**Years 1 and 2**

*Deuteronomy 11.18–28*
The preacher asserts that his words are vital for the future prosperity of the people. They are therefore to be treated with reverence and taught to all Hebrew children. Obedience to the commandments will mean victory in the conquest of the promised land. The passage ends with a blessing and a curse.

*I John 2.22 – end*
John warns his readers against the danger of heresy in their community. He contrasts false and true teaching in terms of the anti-Christ and the Christ. His advice is that Christians should remain true to their baptism and his teaching, and abide in Christ.

*Luke 16.1–9* See Sixteenth Sunday after Pentecost. Second year, evening. Preface for Luke 16.1–13.

# Twenty-third Sunday after Pentecost
(Trinity 22)

The theme and readings for this Sunday are the same as for the Fifth Sunday after Epiphany, though the themes and readings for the First year and the Second year are in reverse order.

## ASB
### Year 1

See Twentieth Sunday after Pentecost. First year, morning.

### Year 2

*Isaiah 33.17–22*  See Twentieth Sunday after Pentecost. Second year, morning.

*Revelation 7.2–4, 9 – end.*
In symbolic language, the prophet describes some features of the days before the end of the present order. He refers to the elect, possibly all Christians, possibly Christian martyrs. Then he records his vision of the worship of God by peoples from every nation. Those who have suffered for their faith have eternal life in the presence of God. The passage is meant to encourage the prophet's contemporaries before they experience the final struggle with evil which the writer expects.

*Matthew 25.1–13*  See Twentieth Sunday after Pentecost. Second year, morning.

# Watchnight

---

## First Year

*Ecclesiastes 3.1–15*
The preacher lists in poetic form various times and seasons and suggests that no human effort is of use, since everything is already determined. His rather cynical reaction is typical of the book of Ecclesiastes, though contrary to the general view found in Jewish scripture, which encourages human effort.

*Luke 12.35–50*
This passage suggests that the disciples of Jesus will be left to take care of his household until he returns from the heavenly banquet; their task is to be vigilant. There is a further illustration of the point in the householder being ready for the thief. The passage contains an indication of Peter's leadership within the early Christian community, for it appears that a particular charge is being given to him to be a faithful steward. In the closing verses Jesus refers to his own death.

## Second year

*Deuteronomy 8.1–20*
The Israelites are urged to learn from their experience of hardship in the wilderness that man does not exist on material things alone, but primarily by God's care, which includes his discipline. This message is addressed to the people enjoying a time of prosperity after settling in Canaan. The writer does not want them to attribute their success either to themselves or to false gods, but rather to acknowledge God as their provider.

*Luke 12.13–21*  See Sixteenth Sunday after Pentecost. First year, evening.

# Aldersgate Sunday
(May 24th or the preceding Sunday)

---

**First year**

*Isaiah 51.1–3, 7–11*
In a message of comfort to the exiles, the prophet reminds the people of God's blessing in the past and promises hope for the future. He therefore calls on the people not to be afraid, but to trust in the deliverance of God. Rahab is the sea-monster thought by the ancients to have preceded the creation of the world.

*Romans 5.1–11*  See Nineteenth Sunday after Pentecost. Second year, morning.

*Mark 12.28–37*
In his reply to a scribe, Jesus combines the basic Jewish law in Deuteronomy, to love God, with the command in the book of Leviticus, to love one's neighbour. This may have been the first time such a combination was made. Certainly it influenced the teaching of the early church. In the last two, and difficult, verses, Jesus refers to his messiahship in relation to a verse from the Psalms.

**Second year**

*Isaiah 12.1–6*  See Easter Day. First year, morning.

*II Peter 1.1–11*  See Twenty-first Sunday after Pentecost. Second year, evening.

*Luke 10.1–12, 17–20*
Luke describes the mission of the seventy followers of Jesus and the instructions given to them for their work. Their central message is the nearness of the kingdom of God, and their reports of what they have done illustrate the power of the kingdom to overcome evil. This story, found only in Luke's Gospel, is seen by the writer as an anticipation of the disciples' mission to the whole world after the resurrection.

# Education Sunday

## First year

*Proverbs 3.13–17*
In this passage, the writer praises wisdom, which he vividly describes as the most precious gift of all and the secret of a happy life.

*Acts 17.16–34*   See Twelfth Sunday after Pentecost. Second year, morning.

*Luke 2.41–52*   See Second Sunday after Christmas. Second year, morning.

## Second year

*Job 28.12–28*   See Ninth Sunday before Easter. Second year, evening.

*I Timothy 4.9–16*
Timothy is reminded of the motive for his ministry and of the various tasks he has to undertake. In particular, he is urged to teach the faith committed to the church and to practise what he preaches.

*Matthew 13.44–58*   See Ninth Sunday before Easter. Second year, evening.

# All Saints' Day

### First year, morning

*Isaiah 66.20–23*
The prophet writes of his hopes for the recognition of God's glory by the whole world and pictures the return of the scattered Jews to Jerusalem.

*Revelation 7.2–4, 9–12*
In his vision, the prophet describes in symbolic language the worship that the whole world will give to God in heaven.

*Matthew 5.1–12* See Ninth Sunday before Easter. First year, morning.

### Second year, morning

*Jeremiah 31.31–34* See Sixth Sunday before Easter. First year, evening.

*Hebrews 12.18–24*
The writer recalls the experience of the Israelites at Mount Sinai, and contrasts their covenant with the new covenant made in Christ. At Mount Sinai, the people experienced dread; at Mount Zion, the new Jerusalem, they experience God's grace. 'The blood of Abel' refers to Genesis 4.10. Abel's blood called for vengeance on Cain; Christ's blood calls for reconciliation.

*Matthew 5.1–12* See Ninth Sunday before Easter. First year, morning.

### First and Second years, evening

*Isaiah 25.1–9*
First, in a psalm of thanksgiving, the prophet recalls God's past mercies to his people. Then he pictures a banquet on Mount Zion, where God is enthroned as Lord of the whole world. Such is the triumph of his rule that even death will be abolished: a rare conviction in Jewish scripture.

*Hebrews 11.32–12.2* See Twenty-first Sunday after Pentecost. First year, morning.

# Remembrance Sunday

**First year**

*II Samuel 23.13–17*   See Ninth Sunday after Pentecost. First year, evening.

*Romans 8.31–35, 37–39*
Paul's experience of God's goodness and love gives him confidence for his Christian life, despite the trials he has to endure. He believes that nothing, not even the spiritual forces in the world, referred to in this passage as principalities and powers, can break the bond between God and his people.

*Matthew 5.1–12*   See Ninth Sunday before Easter. First year, morning;

or *John 15.9–17*   See Fourth Sunday after Pentecost. First year, morning.

**Second year**

*Isaiah 52.7–12*
In a message to those Jews who remained in Jerusalem during the time of exile, the prophet announces the good news that God will restore Jerusalem and that all the world will see his saving work. This proclamation is accompanied by the promise that God will always be with his people.

*Revelation 22.1–5*
The prophet records his vision of a river and a tree, symbols of life in the heavenly city where God will reign for ever. This vision recalls the garden of Eden with its river and its tree of life.

*John 15.9–17*   See Fourth Sunday after Pentecost. First year morning.

# Christian Citizenship Sunday

## First year
*Isaiah 58.1–8*   See Ash Wednesday. First year, morning.

*Romans 14.1–9*
Paul comments on differences of opinion in the church over two particular matters, abstaining from certain foods and keeping the Sabbath. He argues that there should be mutual tolerance within the church and a respect for each other's conscience; for Christians do not live to further their own views, but rather to glorify Christ.

*Matthew 5.43–48*
This passage records the last of the six contrasts found in the Sermon on the Mount between the demand of the law and the response required of a Christian disciple. These contrasts are given as illustrations that the law has been fulfilled in Christ. Here the writer argues that it is better to love an enemy than merely to love one's neighbour.

## Second year

*Amos 5.14–24*
The prophet Amos, speaking at a time of peace and prosperity, attacks the corruption of both the religious and the civil life of the nation. He urges the people to work for a just society. Unless they do this, he warns, the day of judgment will be a time for mourning.

*Romans 13.8–10*
In an echo of the teaching of Jesus, Paul reminds his readers of the supreme importance of love: it is the complete fulfilment of the law.

*Mark 12.13–17*
Mark describes how Jesus avoids the trap set by the Pharisees and the supporters of Herod, who hope to trick him into making a politically compromising statement. Jesus brushes aside the political issue of the recognition of Rome's power and raises the more fundamental question of duty to God.

# Overseas Missions

**First year**

*Isaiah 42.1–9*   See First Sunday after Epiphany. Second year, morning.

*Romans 1.8–17*
Paul addresses the Christians at Rome and states his desire to visit them. In the meantime, he outlines for them the gospel he preaches: the message of God's salvation to all who believe.

*Matthew 16.13–19*
Matthew records Peter's confession that Jesus is the Messiah. The incident illustrates Peter's importance in the early church and indicates the authority he exercised.

**Second year**

*Isaiah 55.6–11*
The prophet calls for repentance and a return to God. He proclaims that God's promised salvation for all people will be achieved.

*Romans 10.5–17*   See Third Sunday before Christmas. Second year, evening.

*John 3.1–16*   See Third Sunday after Epiphany. Second year, evening.

# Harvest Thanksgiving

## First year

*Genesis 8.15–22*
In this conclusion to the ancient story of the flood, the writer recounts what happens when the waters subside. Noah releases the animals from the safety of the ark; then he offers a sacrifice, thanking God for his deliverance. The story closes with God's promise to sustain the order of nature.

*Acts 14.13–17*
Following their healing of a crippled man, Paul and Barnabas have been hailed as gods. Paul condemns such idolatry. He then tells the people about the true God, the creator, who has made himself known through the blessings of nature.

*Mark 4.1–9*
Mark tells the parable of the sower. This parable may reflect Jesus' experience as a teacher, or it may be intended to encourage the disciples in their preaching. In either case, it speaks both of unresponsive hearers and of a great harvest.

## Second year

*Deuteronomy 26.1–11*   See Eighteenth Sunday after Pentecost. First year, morning.

*Timothy 6.6–10*
The writer is concerned to offer guidance to Timothy in his leadership of the church. He says that Christians should be content with the necessities of food and clothing and argues that too much concern with material goods and money brings temptation and ruin.

*Matthew 13.24–33*
Matthew records two parables which compare God's rule to the planting and growth of seeds. The first warns against a premature attempt to distinguish between those people who have responded to God's kingdom and those who have not. The second speaks of

*Harvest Thanksgiving*

growth in the kingdom of God from its small and even hidden
beginnings in the ministry of Jesus. Then follows a parable which
compares the kingdom to the working of leaven.

# Church Anniversary

### First year
*Genesis 28.10–22*   See Nineteenth Sunday after Pentecost. First year, morning.

*Hebrews 10.19–25*
The writer, who is clearly anxious that his readers should not revert to their Jewish faith, describes how Christians are able to offer true worship to God through Christ, who is the high priest in heaven.

*Matthew 21.12–16*
Matthew records how Jesus cleanses the temple and heals there. The story contrasts the reaction of the religious leaders to what Jesus does with that of the children who confirm the greeting given to him at his entry into the city. The passage contains two quotations from the Old Testament.

### Second year

*II Chronicles 7.11–16*
The Chronicler records God's answer to Solomon's prayer at the dedication of the temple in Jerusalem: God promises to dwell in the temple and to hear the people when they call on him in penitence.

*I Peter 2.1–5*
The writer calls on newly-baptized Christians to seek growth in their spiritual lives through their membership of the Christian community, where they can offer to God true worship through Jesus Christ. The writer's description of Christ as a stone leads him to speak of the church as a spiritual building.

*John 10.22–29*
This passage is a continuation of the debate between Jesus and the Jewish leaders. The Jews wish to know who Jesus is, but he replies that, no matter how openly he speaks, those who are not committed to him will not believe. The metaphor of sheep is used to describe believers, because earlier in the chapter Jesus has been called the good shepherd.

## The Transfiguration of our Lord

*Exodus 34.29 – end*   See Third Sunday after Easter. First year, morning.

*II Corinthians 3.4 – end*   See Fifth Sunday after Epiphany. First year, morning. Preface for II Corinthians 3.4–11.

*Luke 9.28–36*   See Third Sunday before Easter. Second year, morning.

## All Saints' Day

*Jeremiah 31.31–34*   See Sixth Sunday before Easter. First year, evening. Preface for Jeremiah 31.27–34.

*II Esdras 2.42 – end*
In a vision, the writer sees the court of heaven in which all are praising God. Each worshipper is crowned by the Son of God as the sign of a faithful confession in the world. This passage is written as a word of encouragement and strength to the faithful.

*Genesis 3.1–15*   See Eighth Sunday before Christmas. First year, morning.

*Hebrews 12.18–24*   See All Saints Day. Second year, morning.

*Revelation 7.2–4, 9 – end*   See Twenty-third Sunday after Pentecost. ASB Year 2.

*Matthew 5.1–12*   See Ninth Sunday before Easter. First year, morning.

*Luke 6.20–23*
Luke opens his account of this sermon, preached by Jesus, with four blessings which will be given to his disciples.

# Festival of the Dedication or Consecration of a Church

*I Kings 8.22–30*
This is an account of the prayer of Solomon at the dedication of the temple in Jerusalem. In building the temple Solomon has fulfilled God's promise to his father, David. He therefore asks that God, whom he knows cannot be contained within the temple, will hear the prayers offered to him there.

*I Peter 2.1–10*   See Second Sunday after Pentecost. First year, morning.

*Matthew 21.12–16*   See Church Anniversary. First year.


*Lesser Festival*

# Harvest Thanksgiving

*Deuteronomy 8.1–10*
The Israelites are urged to learn from their experience of hardship in the wilderness that man does not exist on material things alone, but primarily by God's care, which includes his discipline.

*Genesis 1.1–3, 24–31a*   See Ninth Sunday before Christmas. First year, morning.

*Acts 14.13–17*   See Harvest Thanksgiving. First year.

*I Timothy 6.6–10*   See Harvest Thanksgiving. Second year.

*Luke 12.16–31*
Luke tells the parable of the rich fool. The story warns against covetousness and preoccupation with wordly possessions.

*John 6.27–35*   See Sixth Sunday before Christmas. First year, morning.